Certified in Cybersecurity (CC) Exam

400+ Questions for Guaranteed Success

1st Edition

www.versatileread.com

Copyright © 2024 VERSAtile Reads. All rights reserved.
This material is protected by copyright, any infringement will be dealt with legal and punitive action.

Document Control

Proposal Name	:	Certified in Cybersecurity (CC) Exam: 400+ Questions Guaranteed Success
Document Edition	:	1st
Document Release Date	:	5th September 2024
Reference	:	CC
VR Product Code	:	20243102CC

Copyright © 2024 VERSAtile Reads.

Registered in England and Wales

www.versatileread.com

All rights reserved. No part of this book may be reproduced or transmitted in any form or by any means, electronic or mechanical, including photocopying, recording, or by any information storage and retrieval system, without the written permission from VERSAtile Reads, except for the inclusion of brief quotations in a review.

Feedback:

If you have any comments regarding the quality of this book or otherwise alter it to better suit your needs, you can contact us through email at info@versatileread.com

Please make sure to include the book's title and ISBN in your message.

Voice of the Customer: Thank you for choosing this VersatileRead.com product! We highly value your feedback and insights via email to info@versatileread.com. As a token of appreciation, an amazing discount for your next purchase will be sent in response to your email.

About the Contributor:

Arshamah Sheikh

Arshamah Sheikh is a seasoned content developer with extensive expertise in cloud computing, IT infrastructure, information security, database management, cybersecurity, and Microsoft technologies. She holds certifications in Cisco's NDG Linux Unhatched, Database Design, and Cloud Solution Architecture. With her deep knowledge and professional qualifications, Arshamah excels in creating intuitive, visually appealing content that effectively communicates complex technical concepts.

Table of Contents

About Certified in Cybersecurity (CC) Exam 6
    Introduction 6
    What is (ISC)2? 6
    What is a CC? 6
    What Experience is required to become a CC? 7
    Key Focus Area 7
        Domain 1 – Security Principles 8
        Domain 2 – Business Continuity (BC), Disaster Recovery (DR) and Incident Response Concepts 8
        Domain 3 – Access Controls Concepts 8
        Domain 4 – Network Security 8
        Domain 5 – Security Operations 8
    Exam Information 9
    Job Opportunities with CC Certifications 9
    Benefits of CC Certification 10
    Demand for CC Certification in 2024 11
Practice Questions 12
Answers 89
About Our Products 174

About Certified in Cybersecurity (CC) Exam

Introduction

In today's rapidly evolving digital landscape, the need for cybersecurity professionals is more critical than ever. As organizations grapple with sophisticated cyber threats, having a strong foundation in cybersecurity is essential for defending sensitive information and systems. Enter the Certified in Cybersecurity (CC) certification – a key stepping stone for individuals aspiring to break into the field of cybersecurity.

What is (ISC)2?

The International Information System Security Certification Consortium (ISC)² is an esteemed international nonprofit organization dedicated to certifying and training cybersecurity professionals. They host industry conferences, provide cybersecurity best practices, and offer a range of vendor-neutral certification and training programs. As the certification body for Certified in Cybersecurity (CC), (ISC)² manages the certification process, sets exam requirements, and defines content. Notably, (ISC)² is renowned for its Certified Information Systems Security Professional (CISSP) certification, a global standard for experienced security professionals. Additionally, they administer certifications such as:

- Systems Security Certified Practitioner (SSCP)
- Certified Cloud Security Professional (CCSP)
- Certified in Governance, Risk and Compliance (CGRC)
- Certified Secure Software Lifecycle Professional (CSSLP)
- HealthCare Information Security and Privacy Practitioner (HCISPP)

What is a CC?

CC stands for Certified in Cybersecurity. It is an entry-level certification provided by the International Information System Security Certification Consortium, or (ISC)². CC is recognized for establishing foundational knowledge in cybersecurity, catering to professionals seeking to begin their careers in the field. Individuals pursue CC certification to grasp essential cybersecurity concepts and practices without requiring extensive prior experience. The certification exam typically evaluates knowledge across key domains in cybersecurity over a set duration. CC holders can pursue roles such as Cybersecurity Analyst, Junior Security Consultant, and Security Operations Center (SOC) Analyst. CC-certified professionals prioritize enhancing organizational cybersecurity readiness across various industries.

What Experience is required to become a CC?

No prior experience is required to become Certified in Cybersecurity (CC) from (ISC)². This entry-level certification is suitable for:

- IT professionals who are looking to enter the cybersecurity field.
- Fresh college graduates interested in starting a career in cybersecurity.
- Professionals from other domains who are aiming to transition into cybersecurity roles.

The CC certification is designed to validate foundational knowledge and readiness for cybersecurity responsibilities. It serves as a starting point for those aspiring to advance to more senior cybersecurity certifications and leadership positions within organizations.

Key Focus Area

The Certified in Cybersecurity (CC) certification is an entry-level credential that focuses on foundational cybersecurity concepts. It covers key areas from five specific domains:

About Certified in Cybersecurity (CC) Exam

Domain 1 – Security Principles

- Understanding fundamental security concepts and principles.
- Learning about the CIA triad: confidentiality, integrity, and availability.
- Familiarity with security frameworks and standards.

Domain 2 – Business Continuity (BC), Disaster Recovery (DR) and Incident Response Concepts

- Knowledge of business continuity planning and disaster recovery strategies.
- Understanding the incident response lifecycle and processes.
- Ability to identify, analyze, and respond to security incidents effectively.

Domain 3 – Access Controls Concepts

- Learning different types of access controls and their applications.
- Understanding authentication, authorization, and accountability mechanisms.
- Implementing and managing access controls to protect information systems.

Domain 4 – Network Security

- Knowledge of network structures, devices, and operations.
- Implementing network security controls, protocols, and configurations.
- Learning about firewall management, Intrusion Detection/Prevention Systems (IDS/IPS), and secure network architecture.

Domain 5 – Security Operations

- Understanding the basics of security operations and monitoring.
- Familiarity with security tools and technologies used in day-to-day operations.

About Certified in Cybersecurity (CC) Exam

- Learning to identify and mitigate potential threats and vulnerabilities in security operations.

Exam Information

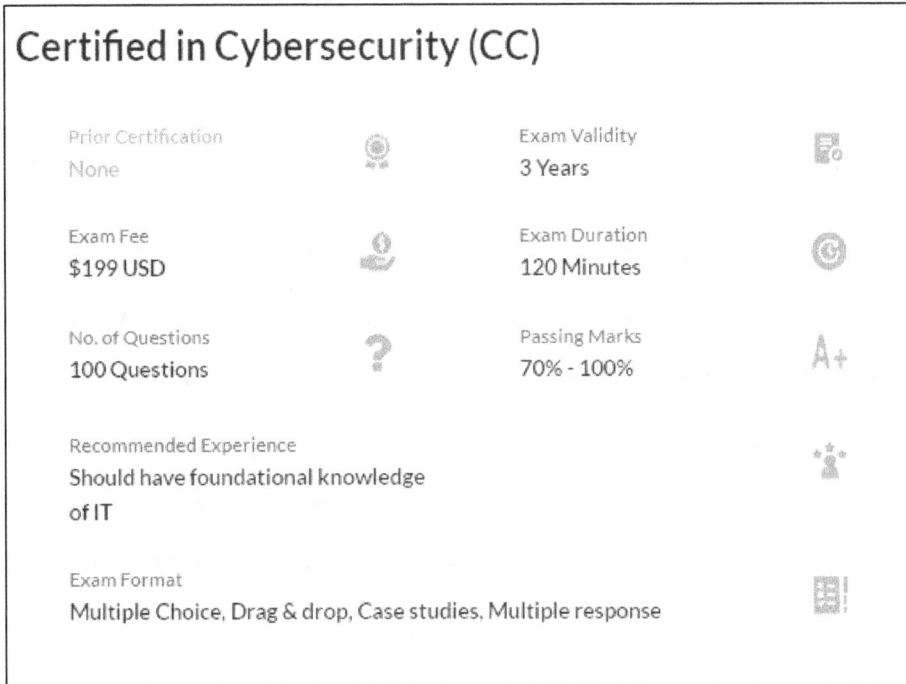

Certified in Cybersecurity (CC)

Prior Certification
None

Exam Validity
3 Years

Exam Fee
$199 USD

Exam Duration
120 Minutes

No. of Questions
100 Questions

Passing Marks
70% - 100%

Recommended Experience
Should have foundational knowledge of IT

Exam Format
Multiple Choice, Drag & drop, Case studies, Multiple response

Job Opportunities with CC Certifications

The Certified in Cybersecurity (CC) certification from (ISC)² is a gateway to diverse career opportunities across industries, equipping professionals with essential skills to navigate today's cybersecurity challenges.

- **Cybersecurity Analyst:** Monitoring and responding to security incidents, conducting risk assessments, and implementing security measures.
- **Security Consultant:** Advising organizations on security strategies, conducting audits, and ensuring compliance with regulatory standards.

About Certified in Cybersecurity (CC) Exam

- **Network Security Engineer:** Designing and maintaining secure network infrastructures, including firewalls and intrusion detection systems.
- **Information Security Specialist:** Protecting information systems through the implementation of security policies and procedures.
- **Incident Response Analyst:** Investigating and mitigating security incidents to minimize organizational risk.
- **Security Operations Center (SOC) Analyst:** Monitoring security alerts, conducting threat analysis, and responding to cyber threats.
- **Security Administrator:** Managing access controls and configurations for IT systems and applications
- **Compliance Analyst:** Ensuring organizational compliance with cybersecurity regulations and standards.
- **Cybersecurity Auditor:** Assessing security controls and practices to identify vulnerabilities and improve security posture.
- **Risk Analyst:** Analyzing cybersecurity risks and developing strategies to mitigate threats to organizational assets.

CC certification demonstrates proficiency in cybersecurity principles, network security, and incident response, making professionals valuable assets in sectors such as finance, healthcare, and government. It provides a solid foundation for entry into the cybersecurity field and opportunities for career advancement.

Benefits of CC Certification

- Specialized Expertise gains deep knowledge of cybersecurity principles.
- Industry Recognition is globally recognized for cybersecurity proficiency.
- Career Advancement access to advanced roles in cybersecurity.
- Niche Opportunities explore specialized areas such as compliance and risk analysis.
- Industry Relevance is crucial in sectors such as finance and healthcare.

About Certified in Cybersecurity (CC) Exam

- Networking is connected with a global community of cybersecurity professionals.

Demand for CC Certification in 2024

The Certified in Cybersecurity (CC) certification is in high demand in 2024 for several compelling reasons:

- With the increasing prevalence of cybercrime, organizations are actively seeking qualified professionals to safeguard their data and systems. The Certified in Cybersecurity (CC) certification validates foundational cybersecurity knowledge, making candidates more competitive in the job market.
- The CC certification is a vendor-neutral credential recognized worldwide. This global recognition makes it a valuable asset for professionals aiming to work in various industries and locations.
- No prior experience is required to pursue the CC certification, making it ideal for IT professionals, career changers, college students, and recent graduates entering the cybersecurity field.
- Covers essential cybersecurity topics, including security principles, network security, incident response, governance, risk, and compliance. This comprehensive coverage equips candidates with a strong foundational understanding of cybersecurity.
- Validates candidates' cybersecurity knowledge, enhancing employability and opening up opportunities for career growth and advancement.
- Provides a solid foundation for pursuing advanced certifications such as CISSP and connects individuals to a network of cybersecurity professionals for continued development and learning.

Practice Questions

Practice Questions

1. What is the primary goal of cybersecurity?
   A. To eliminate all cyber threats
   B. To provide the right amount of protection to each asset based on risks
   C. To increase the speed of information processing
   D. To reduce the cost of information resources

2. How has the role of security evolved from the past to the present?
   A. It has remained the same
   B. It has shifted from physical to digital protection
   C. It has focused more on physical locks and keys
   D. It has become less important

3. Which of the following is an example of a function that depends on information resources?
   A. Cooking
   B. E-mail
   C. Gardening
   D. Traditional banking

4. What is the analogy used to describe the dual nature of cybersecurity?
   A. A book with two chapters
   B. A coin with two sides
   C. A building with two floors
   D. A car with two engines

5. Why do information resources require protection?
   A. They are rarely used
   B. They are vulnerable to attacks
   C. They are expensive
   D. They are difficult to manage

6. What is essential for almost every business and organization?

Practice Questions

A. High-speed internet
B. Robust cybersecurity measures
C. Large physical premises
D. Extensive employee training programs

7. What concept in cybersecurity ensures that only persons with a legitimate need can access a specific resource?
A. Authentication
B. Encryption
C. Need to know
D. Malware detection

8. Why cannot the concept of "need to know" be enforced without authentication?
A. Authentication encrypts data
B. Authentication verifies the user's identity
C. Authentication logs user activities
D. Authentication creates user accounts

9. Which of the following is not a function of authentication?
A. Verifying a user's identity
B. Enforcing the need to know
C. Encrypting data
D. Allowing access to resources

10. What does the process of authentication help to verify?
A. The user's permissions
B. The user's identity
C. The user's activities
D. The user's account balance

11. What is the primary goal of cyber criminals when they attack information systems?
A. To improve system performance
B. To steal assets or disrupt operations

Practice Questions

C. To help organizations improve security
D. To test new software

12. What types of assets are cyber criminals interested in stealing?
A. Physical property
B. Food supplies
C. Money or intellectual property
D. Vehicles

13. What motivations might drive cyber criminals to execute attacks?
A. Personal gain
B. Financial gain
C. Political gain
D. All of the above

14. Who are the typical targets of cyber criminals?
A. Only large corporations
B. Only government agencies
C. Organizations that own and operate information systems
D. Only individuals

15. What is one of the potential impacts of a cyber criminal's attack on an information system?
A. Improved system efficiency
B. Disruption of the system's operation
C. Reduced power consumption
D. Increased internet speed

16. Which of the following is not a goal of cyber criminals?
A. Stealing money
B. Disrupting operations
C. Enhancing system security
D. Stealing intellectual property

Copyright © 2024 VERSAtile Reads. All rights reserved.
This material is protected by copyright, any infringement will be dealt with legal and punitive action.

Practice Questions

17. Cyber criminals' offensive attacks can be categorized as which type of activity?
A. Defensive
B. Offensive
C. Supportive
D. Collaborative

18. What kind of gain is nota motive for cyber criminal activities?
A. Financial gain
B. Political gain
C. Personal gain
D. Charitable gain

19. Which sector might cyber criminals target for intellectual property theft?
A. Agriculture
B. Healthcare
C. Education
D. Information Technology

20. What is the relationship between cyber criminals and the organizations they attack?
A. Collaborative partners
B. Competitors
C. Attackers and targets
D. Service providers

21. What is the primary goal of cybersecurity professionals who carry out cyber defense?
A. To launch cyberattacks
B. To defend against cyberattacks
C. To create new cybersecurity software
D. To monitor internet traffic

Practice Questions

22. Which of the following is not a responsibility of cybersecurity professionals?
A. Defending against cyberattacks
B. Detecting cyberattacks when they occur
C. Responding to and recovering from cyber incidents
D. Developing new hardware for organizations

23. Detecting cyberattacks when they occur falls under which category of responsibilities?
A. Offensive strategies
B. Defensive strategies
C. External strategies
D. Development strategies

24. Which of the following best describes the role of cybersecurity professionals?
A. Offensive attackers
B. Defensive protectors
C. Neutral observers
D. Software developers

25. What do cybersecurity professionals do when a cyber incident occurs?
A. Ignore the incident
B. Respond to and recover from it
C. Delete all data
D. Inform the attackers

26. What is the ultimate goal of detecting cyberattacks?
A. To inform the public
B. To ensure attackers are caught
C. To take preventive measures and respond effectively
D. To create a news story

27. The primary focus of cyber defense is to protect which of the following?
A. Personal computers of employees

Practice Questions

B. The organization as a whole
C. Social media accounts
D. Public relations

28. Which of the following aspects is not mentioned as part of the cyber defense process?
A. Defend against attacks
B. Detect them when they occur
C. Respond to and recover from incidents
D. Develop marketing strategies

29. What are the three core types of protection in cybersecurity known as?
A. CIA triad
B. CAI triad
C. CII triad
D. ACI triad

30. Which of the following is not a part of the CIA triad?
A. Confidentiality
B. Availability
C. Integrity
D. Authentication

31. Which element of the CIA triad focuses on ensuring that data remains accurate and unaltered?
A. Availability
B. Integrity
C. Confidentiality
D. Authenticity

32. What is important for every cybersecurity professional to know about the CIA triad?
A. The order of each protection type
B. The name of the triad
C. The meaning of each leg of the triad

Practice Questions

D. The historical origin of the triad

33. Which of the following best describes 'Integrity' in the CAI triad?
A. Ensuring data can be accessed when needed
B. Ensuring data is encrypted
C. Ensuring data is accurate and unaltered
D. Ensuring data is kept private

34. How do cyber criminals compromise confidentiality?
A. By modifying data
B. By deleting data
C. By accessing data without proper authorization
D. By encrypting data

35. Which of the following methods can protect data against breaches of confidentiality?
A. Regular software updates
B. Physical security measures
C. Access controls
D. Data backups

36. What is the function of access controls in cybersecurity?
A. To ensure data is encrypted
B. To restrict access to data to authorized individuals
C. To monitor network traffic
D. To create backups of data

37. How does cryptography contribute to confidentiality?
A. By making data unreadable to unauthorized persons
B. By ensuring data is always available
C. By making data integrity checks
D. By logging access attempts

38. When does cryptography protect the confidentiality of data?
A. Only when data is in storage

Practice Questions

B. Only when data is being transmitted
C. Both when data is at rest (in storage) and while it is being transmitted
D. Only when data is being processed

39. What does the term "data at rest" refer to?
A. Data being processed by applications
B. Data being transmitted across a network
C. Data stored in storage media
D. Data being displayed on a screen

40. What enables a cryptographic algorithm to perform its function?
A. Plaintext
B. Ciphertext
C. Cryptographic key
D. Encoding techniques

41. Which principle is fundamental to ensuring that information is protected from unauthorized access?
A. Availability
B. Integrity
C. Confidentiality
D. Authentication

42. Why is integrity important in the context of electronically signed contracts?
A. To ensure the data is encrypted
B. To ensure data is accessible
C. To prevent unauthorized changes to the data
D. To reduce the size of the data

43. In the context of data security, what is the result of ensuring data integrity?
A. Data is always accessible
B. Unauthorized users cannot change data
C. Data is encrypted

Practice Questions

D. Data is stored in multiple locations

44. What is the primary purpose of a firewall in network security?
A. Encrypt data
B. Monitor user activity
C. Block unauthorized access
D. Detect malware

45. Who are considered threat actors in the context of information security?
A. System administrators
B. Cyber criminals
C. Software developers
D. Network engineers

46. What are the three main objectives that security controls aim to protect?
A. Speed, efficiency, and cost
B. Confidentiality, integrity, and availability
C. Scalability, compatibility, and usability
D. Design, development, and deployment

47. What is necessary for a computer system to authorize a user?
A. Knowing the user's preferences
B. Knowing the user's identity
C. Knowing the user's age
D. Knowing the user's location

48. Why is it important to protect information assets and resources?
A. To increase system uptime
B. To prevent unauthorized access and threats
C. To reduce power consumption
D. To improve software compatibility

49. What is the role of countermeasures in information security?
A. To authorize user access

Practice Questions

B. To protect against threats
C. To create user accounts
D. To enhance graphic designs

50. What is the relationship between threat actors and information assets?
A. Threat actors protect information assets
B. Threat actors compromise information assets
C. Threat actors are neutral to information assets
D. Threat actors improve information assets

51. What does the principle of "Least Privilege" entail?
A. Granting users the highest level of access they request
B. Providing access based on user roles
C. Giving users only the minimum level of access necessary for their tasks
D. Allowing users to access all resources

52. What is the main goal of Business Continuity Planning (BCP)?
A. To prevent data loss
B. To ensure business operations can continue during and after a disruption
C. To monitor network traffic
D. To manage user access

53. In the context of cybersecurity, what does a system do when it authenticates a user?
A. Creates a backup of all data
B. Verifies that the user is who they claim to be
C. Encrypts all communications
D. Deletes unnecessary files

54. What happens if authentication fails in a cybersecurity system?
A. Access is granted to all users
B. The system crashes
C. The user is denied access
D. The data is backed up automatically

Practice Questions

55. What is the first step a user must go through in the authentication process?
A. Logging in
B. Registration
C. Password reset
D. Multi-Factor Authentication

56. During the registration process, what might users be required to agree to?
A. Privacy policy
B. Terms of service
C. Payment plan
D. User Agreement

57. What kind of physical proof might organizations require during the registration process?
A. Birth certificate
B. Identification card
C. Proof of address
D. Resume

58. When can the organization use any of the types of verification factors to check who a person is?
A. During initial registration
B. Whenever they log in and request access
C. Only during security audits
D. Only during system updates

59. What is the main purpose of the registration process in the authentication system?
A. To assign a username
B. To assert who the user is
C. To create a user profile
D. To generate a password

Practice Questions

60. What does the overall process that authentication fits into entail?
A. Security management
B. User management
C. Access control process
D. Data management process

61. Which of the following statements is most accurate?
A. Security should be done the same way regardless of the situation.
B. Security should be tailored based on the situation.
C. It is always best to mitigate risks rather than transfer them.
D. Risk avoidance trumps security controls every time.

62. What is the ultimate goal of the authentication process?
A. To allow users to reset their passwords
B. To grant access to computing resources
C. To monitor user activity
D. To update user credentials

63. What is the concept of authenticity in information security?
A. The ability to encrypt data
B. The legitimacy of the data transmission
C. The ability to compress data
D. The speed of data transmission

64. What does nonrepudiation in information security ensure?
A. The sender cannot deny sending the data
B. The data is encrypted
C. The data is compressed
D. The data is transmitted quickly

65. Why are authenticity and nonrepudiation important in data transmission?
A. To ensure data is encrypted
B. To ensure data is compressed

Practice Questions

C. To ensure the legitimacy and trustworthiness of the data and transmission process
D. To ensure data is transmitted quickly

66. Which of the following accomplishes authenticity and nonrepudiation?
A. Data compression
B. Encryption only
C. Processes and technologies that prove the identity of the sender and the integrity of the message
D. Increasing transmission speed

67. If a sender denies sending a document, which concept is being challenged?
A. Authenticity
B. Speed
C. Compression
D. Nonrepudiation

68. How can users trust the data and transmission process?
A. By ensuring the data is encrypted
B. By ensuring the data is compressed
C. By verifying the authenticity and nonrepudiation of the data and transmission process
D. By increasing the speed of transmission

69. Which security concept involves monitoring and responding to security incidents?
A. Risk Assessment
B. Security Operations
C. Access Control
D. Cryptography

70. What does nonrepudiation help to verify in data transmission?
A. The encryption method used
B. The compression algorithm

Practice Questions

C. The sender cannot repudiate sending the data
D. The speed of transmission

71. What is the primary objective of an attacker during the 'Identify Targets' phase?
A. To gather financial information
B. To identify an organization's information assets and vulnerabilities
C. To disrupt the organization's communications
D. To steal physical assets

72. What might an attacker produce by using automated tools to probe a target network?
A. Financial statements
B. Lists of target computer systems
C. Employee schedules
D. Marketing strategies

73. What is the purpose of probing further after identifying target computer systems?
A. To gather employee feedback
B. To discover vulnerabilities that could be exploited
C. To improve network performance
D. To enhance software features

74. Which of the following is not a specific target that an attacker might identify?
A. Facilities
B. Data
C. Vendor names
D. Weather patterns

75. What is often the ultimate goal of an attacker when identifying vulnerabilities in an organization's information assets?
A. To improve organizational efficiency
B. To exploit those vulnerabilities

Practice Questions

C. To assist with cybersecurity
D. To sell the information to the organization

76. What might attackers need to create to aid in their attack?
A. Enterprise security guidelines
B. Backup systems
C. Tools
D. User manuals

77. Which of the following is not mentioned as part of the attack process?
A. Designing the attack
B. Creating tools
C. Gaining unauthorized access
D. Notifying the enterprise

78. Internal drivers for a security program include:
A. Compliance requirements
B. Business goals
C. Laws
D. Regulations

79. How is a security program typically managed within an organization?
A. Through external consultants
B. By setting up subprograms or functions
C. By outsourcing to a third party
D. By using only external standards

80. What is the purpose of subprograms within a security program?
A. To address legal issues
B. To manage cybersecurity based on organizational needs
C. To replace internal standards
D. To handle financial audits

81. Security program activities are documented and managed through:
A. Verbal agreements

Practice Questions

B. Policies, procedures, and internal standards
C. External audits only
D. Temporary memos

82. Which of the following is considered an internal standard?
A. Government regulations
B. Industry laws
C. Organizational procedures
D. None of the above

83. The staffing of a security program is part of:
A. External drivers
B. Security governance and management
C. Legal compliance
D. Industry standards

84. What is the relationship between policies, procedures, and internal standards in a security program?
A. They are unrelated elements
B. They are all part of documenting and managing security activities
C. Only policies are important
D. Procedures supersede internal standards

85. What activity results serve as a basis for selecting and implementing security controls in an organization?
A. Financial audits
B. Security governance and risk management
C. Market analysis
D. Employee surveys

86. Which type of assets in an organization are security controls used to protect?
A. Financial assets
B. Physical assets
C. Human resources

Practice Questions

D. Information assets

87. What is the relationship between security governance and security controls?
A. Security controls dictate security governance
B. Security governance and security controls are unrelated
C. Security governance informs the selection of security controls
D. Security controls replace the need for security governance

88. Which of the following does implement security controls typically respond to?

A. Financial audits
B. Risk assessments and governance outcomes
C. Employee performance reviews
D. Customer satisfaction surveys

89. On what should the selection of security controls be based?
A. Market trends
B. Personal opinions of management
C. Structured risk analysis and governance results
D. Historical data on sales

90. What is the primary focus of the organization's activities?
A. Profit maximization
B. Professional ethics
C. Customer satisfaction
D. Market expansion

91. Which of the following best describes the ethical approach of the organization?
A. Doing what is best legally
B. Doing what is best for stakeholders
C. Doing what is best morally
D. Doing what is best for the environment

Practice Questions

92. Which of the following is not emphasized in the organization's activities?
A. Following ethical guidelines
B. Professional ethics
C. Market share growth
D. Moral correctness

93. What ensures that each individual within the organization follows ethical practices?
A. Professional ethics
B. Corporate policies
C. Legal requirements
D. Market competition

94. What does the organization's commitment to ethical standards imply?
A. It focuses solely on legal compliance
B. It prioritizes moral actions
C. It aims for the highest profit margins
D. It primarily targets customer satisfaction

95. Which term best describes the organization's ethical guidelines?
A. Business strategy
B. Professional ethics
C. Corporate governance
D. Market analysis

96. Which of the following is not a term related to risk management?
A. Vulnerabilities
B. Threats
C. Risks
D. Investments

97. What might an organization put in place to defend its assets against risks?
A. Marketing campaigns
B. Security controls

Practice Questions

C. Customer surveys
D. Employee training programs

98. What is a possible structure for overseeing risk management in an organization?
A. Risk oversight board
B. Project management office
C. Sales team
D. Customer service department

99. In some organizations, who might have the responsibility for risk management besides a CRO or CFO?
A. Chief Information Security Officer (CISO)
B. Chief Marketing Officer (CMO)
C. Chief Human Resources Officer (CHRO)
D. Chief Operations Officer (COO)

100. Which of the following best describes a "Zero Trust" security model?
A. Trusting all internal network traffic by default
B. Trusting external network traffic by default
C. Verifying every request, regardless of whether it originates inside or outside the network
D. Only verifying users before granting access to external resources

101. What is the core function of access control?
A. To allow access to all resources
B. To deny access to all resources
C. To allow access to only authorized personnel
D. To allow access to only unauthorized personnel

102. What is the principle of least privilege?
A. Granting users access to all resources
B. Granting users access to only the resources they need
C. Granting users access to more resources than they need
D. Denying users access to all resources

Practice Questions

103. What is the segregation of duties?
A. Assigning multiple tasks to one employee
B. Assigning one task to multiple employees
C. Assigning duties to prevent fraud or errors
D. Assigning duties to cause fraud or errors

104. What is the two-person rule?
A. Requiring one person to perform a function
B. Requiring two people to perform a function
C. Requiring three people to perform a function
D. Requiring four people to perform a function

105. What is a memorized secret?
A. Something you have
B. Something you know
C. Something you are
D. Something you do

106. What is identification in access control?
A. Verifying who you are
B. Proving who you are
C. Providing identifying information
D. Authenticating who you are

107. What is authentication in access control?
A. Verifying who you are
B. Proving who you are
C. Providing identifying information
D. Granting access to resources

108. What is authorization in access control?
A. Verifying who you are
B. Proving who you are
C. Granting access to resources

Practice Questions

D. Providing identifying information

109. What is accountability in access control?
A. Verifying who you are
B. Proving who you are
C. Tracking user actions
D. Granting access to resources

110. What is the purpose of password rotation?
A. To change passwords regularly
B. To keep passwords the same
C. To make passwords stronger
D. To make passwords weaker

111. What is the primary goal of Privileged Access Management (PAM)?
A. To manage regular user accounts
B. To manage privileged accounts and limit their use
C. To grant access to all users
D. To deny access to all users

112. What type of accounts are considered high-risk due to their potential impact?
A. Regular user accounts
B. Privileged accounts
C. Guest accounts
D. Anonymous accounts

113. What principle does PAM apply to decide what types of privileged accounts are necessary?
A. Principle of least privilege
B. Principle of most privilege
C. Principle of equal privilege
D. Principle of no privilege

Practice Questions

114. How many privileged accounts should organizations limit themselves to?
A. As many as possible
B. As few as possible
C. A fixed number
D. An unlimited number

115. What is stored in a separate repository in PAM systems?
A. Credentials for regular user accounts
B. Credentials for privileged accounts
C. Access control lists
D. Authentication protocols

116. In the context of risk management, what does the term "residual risk" refer to?
A. The risk remaining after all mitigation measures have been implemented
B. The risk identified during the initial risk assessment
C. The risk eliminated by security controls
D. The risk that is transferred to a third-party

117. What are the three types of security controls?
A. Administrative, technical, and physical
B. Logical, physical, and administrative
C. Technical, logical, and physical
D. Administrative, logical, and technical

118. What is an example of a technical access control?
A. Locking a door
B. Entering a username and password
C. Installing a firewall
D. Conducting a security audit

119. What is the purpose of logical access controls?
A. To control physical access to resources
B. To control logical access to resources

Practice Questions

C. To ignore access requests
D. To grant access to all users

120. What are the primary types of access control models?
A. DAC, MAC, and RBAC
B. MAC, RBAC, and ABAC
C. DAC, ABAC, and RBAC
D. ABAC, RBAC, and DAC

121. What does DAC stand for?
A. Discretionary Access Control
B. Mandatory Access Control
C. Role-Based Access Control
D. Attribute-Based Access Control

122. Who has full control in a DAC implementation?
A. The security administrator
B. The owner of the resource
C. The user who created the resource
D. The system administrator

123. What is an access control matrix?
A. A table containing a set of subjects, objects, and permissions
B. A list of access control lists
C. A diagram of access control models
D. A report of access control violations

124. What is MAC commonly associated with?
A. Government and military systems
B. Commercial and industrial systems
C. Educational and research systems
D. Personal and home systems

125. What is the purpose of data classification in MAC?
A. To map security requirements to different categories of data

Practice Questions

B. To grant access to all users
C. To deny access to all users
D. To ignore access requests

126. What is RBAC an acronym for?
A. Role-Based Access Control
B. Rule-Based Access Control
C. Relationship-Based Access Control
D. Resource-Based Access Control

127. What is the benefit of RBAC in organizations?
A. It allows customization of permissions for each role
B. It grants access to all users
C. It denies access to all users
D. It ignores access requests

128. What is attribute-based access control also referred to as?
A. Policy-based access control or claims-based access control
B. Role-based access control or identity-based access control
C. Mandatory access control or discretionary access control
D. Logical access control or physical access control

129. Which security control type focuses on preventing security incidents by blocking malicious activity?
A. Detective controls
B. Corrective controls
C. Preventive controls
D. Compensating controls

130. What technologies support identity management?
A. Directories, single sign-on, and federated identity management
B. Firewalls, intrusion detection systems, and encryption
C. Access control lists, authentication protocols, and authorization protocols

Practice Questions

D. Password managers, authentication managers, and authorization managers

131. What is the primary goal of directories in large organizations?
A. To manage physical access
B. To manage logical access
C. To manage administrative access
D. To manage technical access

132. What is Single Sign-On (SSO) in identity management?
A. A technology that requires multiple authentications
B. A technology that allows multiple users to share one account
C. A technology that allows users to access multiple resources after authenticating only once
D. A technology that denies access to all users

133. What is Federated Identity Management (FIM)?
A. A variant of SSO that allows organizations to establish arrangements to utilize different identification and authentication information across multiple organizations
B. A variant of SSO that allows organizations to establish arrangements to utilize the same identification and authentication information across multiple organizations
C. A variant of SSO that denies access to all organizations
D. A variant of SSO that allows access to only one organization

134. What is the purpose of account audits in logical access control?
A. To implement weak passwords
B. To ensure that both privileged/administrator and standard user accounts are regularly reviewed to implement best practices
C. To deny access to all users
D. To grant access to all users

135. What are logical access logs used for?
A. To detect physical attacks

Practice Questions

B. To detect unauthorized access or other attacks by reviewing access events that occur on computers, networks, applications, and other systems
C. To grant access to all users
D. To deny access to all users

136. What are monitoring tools and technologies used for logical access control?
A. To provide automated alerting and/or review of physical access events
B. To provide automated alerting and/or review of access logs and other events
C. To grant access to all users
D. To deny access to all users

137. What is the purpose of physical access controls?
A. To prevent and monitor logical attacks
B. To prevent and monitor physical attacks such as break-ins, theft, and physical harm
C. To grant access to all users
D. To deny access to all users

138. What are perimeter and entrance protection measures used for?
A. To secure facilities by strategically placing physical barriers to prevent and control logical access
B. To secure facilities by strategically placing physical barriers to prevent and control physical access
C. To grant access to all users
D. To deny access to all users

139. What is the purpose of bollards in physical access control?
A. To reduce the risk of someone walking through the entrance
B. To reduce the risk of someone driving a vehicle through the entrance
C. To grant access to all users
D. To deny access to all users

Practice Questions

140. What is the purpose of fencing and walls in physical access control?
A. To restrict access to a physical area and funnel access through approved logical entry points
B. To restrict access to a physical area and funnel access through approved physical entry points
C. To grant access to all users
D. To deny access to all users

141. What are revolving doors and turnstiles used for?
A. To control logical access points by only allowing one person through at a time
B. To control physical access points by only allowing one person through at a time
C. To grant access to all users
D. To deny access to all users

142. What is a mantrap in physical access control?
A. An area with two unlocked doors that must be opened before the second door can be opened
B. An area with two locked doors that must be closed before the second door can be opened
C. An area with one locked door that must be closed before the second door can be opened
D. An area with one unlocked door that must be opened before the second door can be opened

143. What is the most important consideration in physical access control?
A. Protecting the safety of facilities and assets
B. Protecting the safety of employees and people within the organization
C. Granting access to all users
D. Denying access to all users

144. What is fail-secure in physical access control?
A. Doors are configured to open and remain unlocked during a disaster
B. Doors are configured to close and remain locked during a disaster

Practice Questions

C. Doors are configured to open and remain locked during a disaster
D. Doors are configured to close and remain unlocked during a disaster

145. Which of the following is a characteristic of a "black hat" hacker?
A. Engages in ethical hacking for security improvement
B. Focuses on protecting systems and networks
C. Exploits vulnerabilities for personal gain or malicious purposes
D. Operates under strict legal and ethical guidelines

146. What are badge systems used for in-facility access?
A. To validate the identity of people and grant them access to facilities
B. To deny access to all users
C. To grant access to all users
D. To manage physical access

147. What is biometrics technology used for in-facility access?
A. To validate the identity of people and grant them access to facilities
B. To deny access to all users
C. To grant access to all users
D. To manage physical access

148. What is the purpose of access control models in logical access control?
A. To manage physical access
B. To manage administrative access
C. To manage technical access
D. To manage access and implement rules to control how subjects interact with objects

149. In which scenario would you use "Public Key Infrastructure (PKI)"?
A. To secure wireless network communications
B. To manage and distribute encryption keys for digital communications
C. To perform regular system updates and patches
D. To monitor network traffic for anomalies

150. What is another term used for Segregation of Duties?

Practice Questions

A. Division of Responsibilities
B. Distribution of Tasks
C. Separation of Duties
D. Allocation of Roles

151. What does "data masking" achieve in a data security context?
A. Encrypts data during transmission
B. Hides sensitive data in a way that it cannot be reconstructed
C. Manages access permissions to data
D. Monitors data access for unauthorized activities

152. How does the Segregation of Duties help in preventing fraud?
A. By assigning multiple employees to the same task
B. By reducing the total number of tasks
C. By ensuring one employee does not have enough privileges to misuse the system
D. By increasing the workload on each employee

153. Which of the following is an example of Segregation of Duties?
A. One employee writes and signs checks
B. One employee writes checks, and another signs them
C. One employee manages all financial tasks
D. One employee handles all customer service inquiries

154. When do organizations typically use Segregation of Duties?
A. When defining job roles throughout the enterprise
B. Only during financial audits
C. Only in large organizations
D. Only in governmental institutions

155. Which type of job functions are often subjected to Segregation of Duties policies?
A. Incompatible job functions
B. Low-risk job functions
C. Customer service job functions

Practice Questions

D. Creative job functions

156. What potential issues does the Segregation of Duties aim to mitigate?
A. High employee turnover
B. Communication breakdowns
C. Fraud, mistakes, or abuse
D. Inefficiency in work processes

157. What is the outcome if one employee is responsible for both writing and signing checks?
A. Increased productivity
B. Greater job satisfaction
C. Potential for fraud or abuse
D. Improved financial accuracy

158. Why might an organization have policies requiring Segregation of Duties?
A. To comply with governmental regulations
B. To enhance customer service
C. To prevent fraud, mistakes, or abuse
D. To improve marketing strategies

159. How does Segregation of Duties relate to internal controls?
A. It is unrelated to internal controls
B. It is a type of internal control used to prevent fraud or errors
C. It replaces the need for internal controls
D. It complicates internal controls

160. What is the primary purpose of the two-person rule?
A. To increase productivity
B. To reduce the potential for fraud, errors, or abuse
C. To enhance employee collaboration
D. To simplify operations

Practice Questions

161. Which organization implemented the two-person rule in response to Edward Snowden's security breaches?
A. FBI
B. CIA
C. NSA
D. Homeland Security

162. In which critical area does the U.S. government use the two-person rule?
A. Agricultural policies
B. Nuclear weapons controls
C. Educational systems
D. Healthcare management

163. What is a key characteristic of the two-person rule in storage areas?
A. A single lock requiring a password
B. Two locks that require two different people to open
C. Biometric access
D. Digital encryption

164. Which concept is similar to the two-person rule?
A. Redundancy
B. Automation
C. Segregation of duties
D. Centralization

165. What is an example of a sector where the two-person rule is widely used?
A. Retail management
B. Industrial functions requiring added security measures
C. Public relations
D. Customer service

166. What was the profession of Edward Snowden, whose actions prompted the NSA to implement the two-person rule?
A. Government contractor
B. Military officer

Copyright © 2024 VERSAtile Reads. All rights reserved.
This material is protected by copyright, any infringement will be dealt with legal and punitive action.

Practice Questions

C. Politician
D. Cybersecurity analyst

167. What does the two-person rule require for certain functions to be performed?
A. A minimum of one authorized user
B. Automated systems
C. Two authorized users working in tandem
D. External contractors

168. In the context of the two-person rule, what does it mean for functions to be performed "in tandem"?
A. Sequentially, one after another
B. Simultaneously, by two people together
C. Independently, without any collaboration
D. Sporadically, as needed

169. Why might the industry adopt the two-person rule for certain functions?
A. To decrease operational costs
B. To add an extra layer of security
C. To increase the speed of operations
D. To comply with marketing strategies

170. What is the role of "network segmentation" in enhancing security?
A. To ensure data is encrypted during transmission
B. To divide a network into smaller, isolated segments to limit the spread of attacks
C. To monitor network traffic for suspicious activity
D. To authenticate users accessing the network

171. Which of the following is an example of a memorized secret?
A. Fingerprint
B. Facial recognition

Practice Questions

C. Password
D. RFID card

172. Memorized secrets are used to:
A. Encrypt data
B. Authenticate a user
C. Backup data
D. Monitor network traffic

173. What types of sequences can passwords consist of?
A. Only numbers
B. Only letters
C. Numbers, letters, or characters
D. Only special characters

174. Lock combinations can be:
A. Only numbers
B. Numbers, letters, or characters
C. Only letters
D. Only symbols

175. Who knows the memorized secret?
A. The system administrator
B. The user
C. The IT department
D. Everyone in the organization

176. What verifies that the authorized user is the one requesting access?
A. Correct entry of the memorized secret
B. IP address verification
C. MAC address filtering
D. Security question

Practice Questions

177. Which method is most effective for protecting sensitive data from unauthorized access while maintaining its usability for application development and testing?
A. Data Encryption
B. Data Masking
C. Data Backup
D. Data Redaction

178. Which of the following would not be considered a memorized secret?
A. Password
B. Lock combination
C. Security token
D. PIN

179. For what purpose is the correct entry of a password or combination used?
A. To encrypt data
B. To verify the user's identity
C. To generate reports
D. To access the network

180. What are the two fundamental types of computer networks?
A. Ethernet and Wi-Fi
B. Local Area Network (LAN) and Wide Area Network (WAN)
C. Wired and Wireless
D. Public and Private

181. Which IEEE standard defines Ethernet?
A. 802.11
B. 802.15
C. 802.3
D. 802.16

182. What is the primary purpose of a MAC address?
A. To route traffic over the internet

Practice Questions

B. To identify devices on the same LAN
C. To encrypt data
D. To define a device's IP address

183. What does the term SSID refer to in wireless networks?
A. A security protocol
B. A network's name
C. A type of router
D. A type of switch

184. Which layer of the OSI model do MAC addresses operate at?
A. Layer 1
B. Layer 2
C. Layer 3
D. Layer 4

185. What is the difference between static and dynamic IP addresses?
A. Static IP addresses change over time, while dynamic IP addresses do not
B. Static IP addresses are manually configured, while dynamic IP addresses are assigned automatically
C. Static IP addresses are public, while dynamic IP addresses are private
D. Static IP addresses are used in LANs, while dynamic IP addresses are used in WANs

186. What is a router's primary function?
A. To connect devices within the same LAN
B. To route data between network segments
C. To assign IP addresses
D. To encrypt network traffic

187. What is the purpose of a switch in a network?
A. To route traffic based on IP addresses
B. To physically segment parts of the network
C. To assign MAC addresses
D. To provide wireless connectivity

Practice Questions

188. What type of network device is described as a "multiport repeater"?
A. Switch
B. Router
C. Hub
D. Firewall

189. Which protocol suite is commonly used in modern networks?
A. HTTP
B. FTP
C. TCP/IP
D. SMTP

190. What is the primary role of a firewall in a network?
A. To assign IP addresses
B. To route traffic between networks
C. To enforce security rules governing traffic flow
D. To provide wireless connectivity

191. What is the primary difference between a LAN and a WAN?

A. LAN covers a limited geographic area, while WAN covers a wide geographic area
B. LAN is wired, while WAN is wireless
C. LAN uses MAC addresses, while WAN uses IP addresses
D. LAN is public, while WAN is private

192. Which device allows wireless-capable devices to connect to a network?
A. Router
B. Switch
C. Hub
D. Wireless Access Point

193. What is the role of DHCP in a network?
A. To assign MAC addresses

Practice Questions

B. To assign IP addresses dynamically
C. To route traffic
D. To encrypt data

194. What does VLAN stand for?
A. Virtual Local Area Network
B. Virtual Large Area Network
C. Visual Local Area Network
D. Visual Large Area Network

195. What type of device is typically used to physically segment parts of a network?
A. Router
B. Switch
C. Hub
D. Firewall

196. Which of the following best describes an endpoint in a network?
A. A device that routes traffic
B. A computing device on the network
C. A device that assigns IP addresses
D. A security device

197. What is the function of NAT in a home router?
A. To assign IP addresses
B. To translate private IP addresses to public IP addresses
C. To route traffic within the LAN
D. To provide wireless connectivity

198. What is the smallest unit of information in networking?
A. Byte
B. Bit
C. Kilobyte
D. Megabyte

Practice Questions

199. What is the role of protocols in network communication?
A. To assign IP addresses
B. To route traffic between networks
C. To establish rules and standards for communication
D. To physically connect devices

200. Which of the following protocols is considered secure for transmitting data?
A. HTTP
B. SSL/TLS
C. FTP
D. Telnet

201. What is the primary method used to protect data in transit?
A. Compression
B. Encryption
C. Duplication
D. Obfuscation

202. What does SSL/TLS stand for?
A. Secure Shell and Transport Layer Security
B. Secure Sockets Layer and Transport Layer Security
C. Secure Sockets Layer and Transmission Layer Security
D. Secure Sockets Layer and Tunnel Layer Security

203. Which protocol is used to secure HTTP?
A. SSH
B. SSL/TLS
C. FTP
D. SMTP

204. What happens to data when it is encrypted?
A. It becomes larger
B. It becomes unreadable and turns into ciphertext
C. It is compressed to save space

Practice Questions

D. It is duplicated for redundancy

205. Which of the following is an example of a nonsecure protocol?
A. HTTPS
B. SSH
C. HTTP
D. SFTP

206. What type of attacks does SSL/TLS help prevent?
A. Phishing
B. SQL Injection
C. Man-in-the-middle
D. Brute force

207. What is the primary concern when transmitting data across a network?
A. Speed
B. Bandwidth
C. Security
D. Latency

208. Which protocol is typically used for secure remote command-line access?
A. FTP
B. Telnet
C. SSH
D. HTTP

209. What does HTTPS stand for?
A. Hypertext Transfer Protocol Simple
B. Hypertext Transmission Protocol Secure
C. Hypertext Transfer Protocol Secure
D. Hypertext Transfer Protocol Server

210. What is a logical port?
A. A physical connector on a computer

Practice Questions

B. A numerical identifier mapped to a protocol
C. A type of malware
D. A file extension

211. Which control mechanism is typically used to ensure that actions performed on data are properly recorded and auditable?
A. Access Control
B. Data Encryption
C. Logging and Monitoring
D. Intrusion Detection Systems

212. How is a port similar to a phone extension?
A. Both are used to store data
B. Both identify a specific service or individual on a larger network
C. Both are physical devices
D. Both are types of IP addresses

213. What combination is commonly referred to as a socket?
A. IP address and hardware address
B. Port number and hardware address
C. Port number and IP address
D. Protocol and data packet

214. In a "Zero Trust" architecture, what principle is fundamental for validating each request?
A. Trust but Verify
B. Least Privilege
C. Network Segmentation
D. Always Verify, Never Trust

215. Why are different port numbers assigned to different services on a server?
A. To allow the server to charge different rates for different services
B. To allow a single IP to receive different communication requests
C. To increase the physical security of the server

Practice Questions

D. To monitor the performance of the server

216. What does the client use to specify which service they want to interact with on a server?
A. The server's physical address
B. The server's MAC address
C. The server's port number
D. The server's operating system

217. If a computer functions as both a web server and a file transfer server, what would it need to distinguish between the two services?
A. Different IP addresses for each service
B. Different operating systems for each service
C. Different port numbers for each service
D. Different physical servers for each service

218. What type of risk management strategy involves transferring the risk to a third party?
A. Risk Mitigation
B. Risk Avoidance
C. Risk Acceptance
D. Risk Transfer

219. What is the main objective of a "Security Operations Center (SOC)" in an organization?
A. To develop new security policies and procedures
B. To manage and oversee compliance with regulations
C. To monitor, detect, and respond to security incidents in real-time
D. To design and implement encryption protocols

220. What does the term "Attack Surface" refer to in cybersecurity?
A. The number of physical entry points to a network
B. The total number of vulnerabilities in a system
C. The sum of all potential points where an attacker could exploit a system
D. The security measures implemented to protect a network

Practice Questions

221. Which regulatory framework is focused on protecting personal data in the European Union?
A. HIPAA
B. SOX
C. GDPR
D. FISMA

222. What is the purpose of implementing "Network Segmentation" in an organization's security strategy?
A. To isolate sensitive data from the public network
B. To reduce the attack surface and contain potential breaches within specific segments
C. To improve network speed and performance
D. To enforce encryption protocols for data transmission

223. Which of the following is a common method for validating the integrity of data?
A. Data Encryption
B. Hashing
C. Data Masking
D. Access Control

224. In the context of threat modeling, which method involves identifying and assessing potential threats by understanding the attacker's perspective?
A. Attack Trees
B. STRIDE
C. PASTA
D. OCTAVE

225. What type of attack leverages the trust relationship between a user's browser and a website to execute malicious scripts?
A. Cross-Site Scripting (XSS)
B. Cross-Site Request Forgery (CSRF)
C. SQL Injection

Copyright © 2024 VERSAtile Reads. All rights reserved.
This material is protected by copyright, any infringement will be dealt with legal and punitive action.

Practice Questions

D. Buffer Overflow

226. Which security framework provides a structured approach to managing security controls across various IT systems and is widely used in regulatory compliance?
A. NIST Cybersecurity Framework (CSF)
B. ISO/IEC 27001
C. COBIT
D. PCI-DSS

227. Which layer of the OSI model is responsible for routing and route selection for network packets?
A. Physical Layer
B. Data Link Layer
C. Network Layer
D. Transport Layer

228. What devices are most commonly associated with the Network Layer?
A. Hubs
B. Switches
C. Routers
D. Modems

229. What type of switch has routing capabilities and operates at the Network Layer?
A. Layer 1 switch
B. Layer 2 switch
C. Layer 3 switch
D. Layer 4 switch

230. Which protocol is not associated with the Network Layer?
A. IP
B. ICMP
C. TCP
D. Routing protocols

Practice Questions

231. The Network Layer primarily uses which type of addresses for routing?
A. MAC addresses
B. Logical IP addresses
C. Physical addresses
D. None of the above

232. What is the primary function of the Network Layer in the OSI model?
A. Error detection
B. Data encryption
C. Routing and route selection
D. Data encapsulation

233. Which of the following devices does not operate at the Network Layer?
A. Router
B. Layer 3 switch
C. Hub
D. None of the above

234. Which of the following protocols is used for error reporting and diagnostics in the Network Layer?
A. IP
B. ICMP
C. TCP
D. UDP

235. What is the main purpose of routing protocols at the Network Layer?
A. To encrypt data
B. To select the best path for data transmission
C. To manage physical connections
D. To provide application services

236. What type of vulnerability is associated with improper handling of user input that allows an attacker to execute arbitrary commands on a system?
A. Command Injection

Practice Questions

B. Directory Traversal
C. Cross-Site Request Forgery (CSRF)
D. SQL Injection

237. What is the primary responsibility of the Data Link Layer?
A. Routing packets across networks
B. Transmitting and delivery of frames within a LAN
C. Managing user sessions
D. Encrypting data for security

238. The Data Link Layer is made up of how many sublayers?
A. One
B. Two
C. Three
D. Four

239. Which of the following protocols operates at the Data Link Layer?
A. TCP
B. IP
C. ARP
D. HTTP

240. What does LLC stand for in the context of the Data Link Layer?
A. Logical Link Communication
B. Local Link Control
C. Logical Link Control
D. Local Link Communication

241. Which IEEE standard corresponds to wireless Ethernet?
A. IEEE 802.3
B. IEEE 802.5
C. IEEE 802.11
D. IEEE 802.15

Practice Questions

242. In an incident response process, what is the primary objective of the "Containment" phase?
A. To identify the root cause of the incident
B. To restore systems to normal operations
C. To limit the spread of the incident and prevent further damage
D. To document the incident for future reference

243. What concept involves using redundant systems and components to ensure continuous operation in the event of a failure?
A. High Availability
B. Load Balancing
C. Fault Tolerance
D. Disaster Recovery

244. What role does the MAC sublayer play in the Data Link Layer?
A. Encryption of data
B. Defining physical MAC addresses
C. Managing user sessions
D. Routing packets

245. Which of the following is not a standard or protocol that operates at the Data Link Layer?
A. Ethernet (IEEE 802.3)
B. IP
C. ARP
D. Wireless Ethernet (IEEE 802.11)

246. Which cryptographic algorithm is designed to securely generate and exchange symmetric keys over an insecure channel?
A. RSA
B. AES
C. Diffie-Hellman
D. SHA-256

Practice Questions

247. Which protocol is commonly used for remotely logging into Unix/Linux computers?
A. FTP
B. HTTP
C. SSH
D. SMTP

248. What type of interface does SSH provide for interaction with Unix/Linux computers?
A. Graphical User Interface (GUI)
B. Text-only command-line interface
C. Web-based Interface
D. Voice Command Interface

249. Which port does SSH typically run over?
A. 21
B. 22
C. 23
D. 25

250. Which protocol should SSH be leveraged over due to its lack of security?
A. FTP
B. HTTP
C. Telnet
D. SMTP

251. What does IoT stand for?
A. Internet of Technology
B. Internet of Things
C. Internet of Tools
D. Internet of Tactics

252. Why are IoT devices often called smart devices?
A. They are very expensive

Practice Questions

B. They contain processing capability combined with sensors and automation
C. They are difficult to hack
D. They are only used in homes

253. Which of the following is not a common application of IoT devices?
A. Home automation
B. Manufacturing control systems
C. Medical and healthcare
D. Traditional desktop computing

254. What is a common security vulnerability in IoT devices?
A. Strong encryption
B. Weak authentication mechanisms
C. Built-in antivirus software
D. Robust firewalls

255. Which of the following is a compensating control for IoT devices?
A. Weak passwords
B. Changing default settings
C. Poor authentication
D. Lack of security features on the interface

256. Why is physical access a security issue for IoT devices?
A. IoT devices are always used indoors
B. Many IoT devices are deployed in environments where physical security is challenging
C. IoT devices are immune to physical tampering
D. IoT devices do not require physical security

257. What is the primary purpose of a security program assessment?
A. To hack into the organization's network
B. To evaluate the effectiveness of an organization's security program
C. To install new security software
D. To replace outdated hardware

Practice Questions

258. Who often performs security assessments and testing in organizations?
A. Only in-house staff
B. Independent auditors or third-party firms
C. Only the CEO
D. External law enforcement

259. Which of the following is not typically part of a security program assessment?
A. Regulatory compliance review
B. Network security review
C. Physical security review
D. Installing new hardware

260. Which of the following techniques is used to ensure the confidentiality of data in a cloud environment where multiple tenants share the same infrastructure?
A. Encryption at Rest
B. Data Masking
C. Multi-Factor Authentication
D. Access Control Lists

261. What are the two main types of data center infrastructure models?
A. Local and remote
B. On-premises and cloud
C. Wired and wireless
D. Public and private

262. What is the key difference between on-premises and cloud infrastructure?
A. On-premises is always more secure
B. Cloud infrastructure is always cheaper
C. The way services are provisioned, managed, and utilized
D. On-premises infrastructure does not need physical security

Practice Questions

263. Which role is not typically associated with managing an on-premises data center?
A. Facilities manager
B. Safety officer
C. IT personnel
D. Marketing manager

264. What does HVAC stand for in the context of data center environmental protection?
A. High Voltage and Air Conditioning
B. Heating, Ventilation, and Air Conditioning
C. High Velocity Air Control
D. Heating and Vapor Control

265. Why is network redundancy important in a data center?
A. It reduces costs
B. It ensures continuous network connectivity in case of an issue
C. It makes the network slower
D. It eliminates the need for security

266. What is a common method of achieving power redundancy in data centers?
A. Using a single power line
B. Installing solar panels
C. Using batteries and electric generators
D. Having no backup power system

267. Which component is typically not included in a security program assessment?
A. Security policy review
B. Data security review
C. Social media strategy review
D. Incident handling review

268. What is the main goal of penetration testing?

Practice Questions

A. To identify new business opportunities
B. To show how vulnerabilities can be exploited
C. To improve customer service
D. To increase the number of network devices

269. Which of the following is not a type of vulnerability assessment?
A. Network and system vulnerability testing
B. Application security assessment
C. Physical security assessment
D. Marketing vulnerability assessment

270. What should be included in an organization's security policies regarding IoT devices?
A. Allowing all default settings
B. Ignoring IoT devices
C. Addressing IoT usage, configuration, and security testing
D. Disabling all IoT devices in the network

271. What is a critical component of maintaining the continuity of ongoing data center operations?
A. High-performance computing
B. Data encryption
C. Redundancy of supply systems
D. User training programs

272. Which of the following should organizations have in place to ensure timely replacement and restoration of services in case of an outage?
A. Marketing plans
B. Service level agreements
C. Software updates
D. Training sessions

273. Which process is used to analyze and document the level of redundancy required by an organization?
A. Risk assessment

Practice Questions

B. Business impact analysis
C. Network topology
D. Data encryption

274. What does hardware redundancy in a data center typically involve?
A. Software backups
B. Firewall configurations
C. Backup hardware components
D. Cloud storage solutions

275. Which is not a factor that might cause a power outage in a data center?
A. Severe weather
B. Equipment failure
C. Software malfunction
D. Physical damage to power systems

276. What is the purpose of an Uninterruptible Power Supply (UPS) in a data center?
A. To manage network traffic
B. To provide a short window of power until backup systems activate
C. To enhance data encryption
D. To monitor user activity

277. Which type of facility agreement allows organizations to aid each other during disasters?
A. Sales contracts
B. Reciprocal agreements
C. Marketing alliances
D. Software licenses

278. What is the role of preventative maintenance in data center operations?
A. To reduce system performance
B. To enhance data encryption
C. To ensure systems run smoothly and reduce outage chances
D. To decrease user access

Practice Questions

279. What does NIST define cloud computing as?
A. A way to improve data encryption
B. A method for automating user access
C. A model for enabling on-demand network access to a shared pool of computing resources
D. A protocol for managing software updates

280. Which cloud computing characteristic allows customers to configure resources as needed?
A. Broad network access
B. Measured service
C. On-demand self-service
D. Resource pooling

281. In which cloud service model does the customer manage the OS, applications, and platforms?
A. IaaS
B. PaaS
C. SaaS
D. IDaaS

282. What does the term "multitenancy" describe in the context of cloud computing?
A. Multiple users sharing the same operating system
B. Allocation of cloud resources to multiple tenants while keeping their data isolated
C. Use of multiple cloud providers by one organization
D. Combining public and private cloud resources

283. Which type of cloud deployment model is exclusive to a single organization?
A. Public cloud
B. Community cloud
C. Hybrid cloud

Practice Questions

D. Private cloud

284. What does the term "Security Posture" refer to in an organization's cybersecurity strategy?
A. The overall effectiveness of an organization's security controls and policies
B. The physical security measures in place at a facility
C. The responsiveness of the IT department to security incidents
D. The specific configuration of network devices and firewalls

285. What is the purpose of a Service Level Agreement (SLA)?
A. To improve user training
B. To define the level of service and metrics for a service provider
C. To manage software licenses
D. To establish marketing strategies

286. Which SOC audit type focuses on security and privacy controls?
A. SOC 1
B. SOC 2
C. SOC 3
D. SOC 4

287. What is a characteristic of a hybrid cloud deployment model?
A. Resources are used by a single organization
B. It is only available to the general public
C. It combines two or more different cloud models
D. It is exclusively managed by a third party

288. What is the primary concern organizations have when utilizing a CSP?
A. Cost of services
B. Implementation of good security practices
C. User accessibility
D. Availability of software updates

289. What does a SOC 1 audit assess?

Practice Questions

A. Financial controls
B. Security controls
C. Privacy controls
D. Marketing strategies

290. Which characteristic of cloud computing involves the rapid scaling of resources?
A. On-demand self-service
B. Rapid elasticity
C. Resource pooling
D. Broad network access

291. What is the primary purpose of the CSA STAR program?
A. To provide a comprehensive set of guidelines for software development
B. To enable Cloud Service Providers (CSPs) to document the security controls they offer with their cloud services
C. To offer training and certification programs for cloud security professionals
D. To provide a marketplace for cloud services

292. What resource can Cloud Service Customers (CSCs) use to find CSPs and their corresponding assurance levels in the CSA STAR program?
A. CSA STAR Framework
B. CSA STAR Certification Guide
C. CSA STAR Registry
D. CSA STAR Documentation

293. What is the first phase of the data lifecycle?
A. Data Analysis
B. Data Creation
C. Data Archival
D. Data Destruction

294. How can an organization acquire data?
A. Through internal creation only

Practice Questions

B. Only from a vendor
C. From another organization or created internally
D. Through data destruction

295. Which of the following is a key consideration when data comes to exist within an organization?
A. Data Deletion
B. Appropriate data protection
C. Data Transformation
D. Data Visualization

296. What is an example of an appropriate data protection method?
A. Data Transformation
B. Encryption
C. Data Deletion
D. Data Visualization

297. Which of the following is not a method of protecting data?
A. Access Controls
B. Data Monitoring
C. Data Sharing
D. Encryption

298. When data comes to exist, what must an organization consider regarding privacy?
A. How data may be used and shared
B. How data may be deleted
C. How data may be transformed
D. How data may be visualized

299. What should be monitored to ensure data protection?
A. Data Sharing
B. Data Access
C. Data Deletion
D. Data Analysis

Practice Questions

300. What is necessary to control who can access data?
A. Data Visualization
B. Access Controls
C. Data Sharing
D. Data Deletion

301. Which phase involves the decision on how to protect data?
A. Data Destruction
B. Data Archival
C. Data Creation
D. Data Analysis

302. Why is it important to consider privacy requirements in data management?
A. To ensure data is always available
B. To comply with legal and ethical standards
C. To transform data efficiently
D. To visualize data effectively

303. What is the primary purpose of data classification in organizations?
A. To categorize data for easier retrieval
B. To control and protect different kinds of data
C. To reduce storage costs
D. To enhance data analytics

304. What determines the classification level assigned to a data type?
A. The size of the data
B. The age of the data
C. The risk associated with the data
D. The format of the data

305. Which of the following is an example of a high sensitivity classification level?
A. Public

Practice Questions

B. Unrestricted
C. Top Secret
D. Archived

306. What dictates the controls used to protect classified data?
A. The data format
B. The classification level
C. The data owner
D. The geographical location of the data

307. How is classified data typically marked within an organization?
A. By using different file formats
B. By using encryption algorithms
C. By labeling and tagging
D. By compressing the data

308. What is one method mentioned for labeling physical media?
A. Using barcodes
B. Using encryption
C. Using tags
D. Using stickers

309. Which level of data classification would likely require the most stringent access controls?
A. Public
B. Company Proprietary
C. Unrestricted
D. Archived

310. What does data classification help to ensure about sensitive data?
A. It is publicly accessible
B. It is appropriately protected and only accessible by those with proper authorization
C. It is easily editable by all employees
D. It is stored in the cloud

Practice Questions

311. Which of the following is not a possible action taken after classifying data?
A. Encrypting the data
B. Deleting the data
C. Monitoring access to the data
D. Applying access controls

312. What is a likely consequence of not properly labeling classified data?
A. Increased storage costs
B. Data being accessed by unauthorized individuals
C. Faster data retrieval
D. Reduced data redundancy

313. Data security aims to protect information important to which of the following?
A. General public
B. Organization
C. Government
D. Media

314. Which of the following is not an example of information that may require protection?
A. Employee records
B. Public news articles
C. Sensitive customer data
D. Confidential company information

315. What does data security aim to protect information against?
A. Unauthorized access, modification, and disclosure
B. Natural disasters
C. Hardware malfunctions
D. Software updates

Practice Questions

316. Which of the following are considered technical measures in data security controls?
A. Training programs
B. Computer hardware and software
C. Legal regulations
D. Market analysis

317. Who needs to be aware of the three key data security practices?
A. (ISC)2 CC candidates
B. General public
C. Media professionals
D. Marketing team

318. What type of records is considered as information that requires protection?
A. Media reports
B. Employee records
C. Public directories
D. Weather forecasts

319. Which term best describes data security controls?
A. Technical measures
B. Legal documents
C. Financial investments
D. Marketing strategies

320. What is the primary focus of data security practices?
A. Profit maximization
B. Information protection
C. Product development
D. Customer satisfaction

321. What type of information is classified as "confidential company information"?
A. Public news articles

Practice Questions

B. Intellectual property
C. Weather forecasts
D. Stock prices

322. What must be implemented to protect sensitive information?
A. Data security controls
B. Branding strategies
C. Market research
D. Customer surveys

323. What is the purpose of archiving data?
A. To permanently delete it
B. To keep it for future use or legal requirements
C. To make it accessible for everyday operations
D. To enhance data processing speed

324. Which of the following is not considered as a type of data archival media?
A. Tape
B. Disk
C. Optical media
D. Flash drive

325. What is data retention?
A. The process of deleting unnecessary data
B. The process of storing data that is no longer needed in production but needs to be kept
C. The process of creating data backups
D. The process of encrypting sensitive data

326. Why might an organization need to retain data even if it is no longer needed?
A. To improve system performance
B. To comply with legal requirements
C. To reduce storage costs

Practice Questions

D. To simplify data management

327. Data archival can be implemented using:
A. Only on-premises solutions
B. Only cloud solutions
C. Both on-premises and cloud solutions
D. Only physical storage solutions

328. Which of the following is true about data retention laws?
A. They are only applicable at the federal level
B. They require organizations to delete data immediately after use
C. They mandate organizations to retain data for certain periods
D. They only apply to digital data

329. What happens to data that is no longer needed by an organization but must be stored?
A. It is permanently deleted
B. It is archived
C. It is encrypted and kept in the production environment
D. It is moved to a database

330. Which vulnerability management approach involves regularly scanning for vulnerabilities and implementing fixes or mitigations as part of a continuous improvement process?
A. Penetration Testing
B. Vulnerability Assessment
C. Security Auditing
D. Risk Management

331. What is one of the main purposes of data archival?
A. To make data easily accessible for everyday operations
B. To meet legal and regulatory data retention requirements
C. To reduce data redundancy
D. To enhance data analytics

Practice Questions

332. Can data archival be performed using cloud implementations?
A. Yes
B. No
C. Only for certain types of data
D. Only if legal requirements allow

333. What happens when you delete data by pressing the DELETE key on a computer?
A. The data is permanently removed from the hard drive
B. The data is moved to the recycle bin
C. The data is marked as available for future use
D. The data is overwritten immediately

334. What does emptying the recycle bin on your desktop do to the data on the hard drive?
A. Permanently erases the data from the hard drive.
B. Marks the location as available for future use.
C. Overwrites the data with random values.
D. Encrypts the data for security.

335. Which of the following actions can easily recover data that has been deleted or emptied from the recycle bin?
A. Using free data recovery tools.
B. Overwriting the data.
C. Degaussing the media.
D. Physically destroying the media.

336. What is the term used to describe the process of making sure that sensitive data cannot be recovered from media?
A. Erasure
B. Sanitization
C. Encryption
D. Compression

337. Which of the following is a method of sanitization?

Practice Questions

A. Moving data to the recycle bin
B. Overwriting
C. Compressing the data
D. Encrypting the data

338. What does overwriting involve in the context of data sanitization?
A. Encrypting the data so it cannot be read
B. Writing new data over the old data
C. Physically destroying the media
D. Moving the data to a secure location

339. Which sanitization method uses magnetic fields to erase data?
A. Overwriting
B. Degaussing
C. Compression
D. Encryption

340. What is the primary requirement when data is no longer needed?
A. Compressing the data to save space
B. Ensuring sensitive data cannot be recovered
C. Encrypting the data for security
D. Moving the data to a secure location

341. What does the physical destruction of media involve?
A. Shredding or breaking the media into pieces
B. Overwriting the data multiple times
C. Moving the data to a different location
D. Encrypting the data so it cannot be accessed

342. Which of the following is not a method of sanitization?
A. Overwriting
B. Degaussing
C. Physical destruction
D. Moving data to the recycle bin

Practice Questions

343. In the context of network security, what does the term "Firewall Rule Set" refer to?
A. A collection of encryption algorithms used by a firewall
B. The physical hardware configuration of a firewall
C. The set of rules defining which network traffic is allowed or denied by a firewall
D. The procedure for updating firewall firmware

344. What term is used to describe the act of replacing data with binary 1's and 0's or other patterns?
A. Decryption
B. Encryption
C. Zeroization
D. Compression

345. Which of the following is not a method used for overwriting data?
A. Using other data
B. Using patterns
C. Using random data
D. Using color codes

346. How does increasing the number of passes in data overwriting affect data recovery?
A. Makes the original data easier to recover
B. Makes the original data harder to recover
C. Does no effect on data recovery
D. Changes the format of the original data

347. What does the term "pass" refer to in the context of data overwriting?
A. The speed of data access
B. A single instance of data being overwritten
C. The size of the data being overwritten
D. The type of data being used for overwriting

Practice Questions

348. Why might random data be used in the process of overwriting?
A. To increase storage capacity
B. To make the overwriting process faster
C. To ensure the original data is harder to recover
D. To reduce power consumption

349. Which is a more secure method of data overwriting, a single pass or multiple passes?
A. A single pass
B. Multiple passes
C. Both are equally secure
D. Neither is secure

350. What is another term for zeroization in the context of data overwriting?
A. Data encryption
B. Data compression
C. Data clearing
D. Data sorting

351. What is likely to happen if data is overwritten only once?
A. The original data will be impossible to recover
B. The original data may still be recoverable
C. The original data will be encrypted
D. The data access speed will increase

352. Data overwriting is primarily concerned with which aspect of data management?
A. Data security
B. Data structure
C. Data accessibility
D. Data visualization

353. What is the process of transforming plaintext into ciphertext called?
A. Decryption
B. Encryption

Practice Questions

C. Encoding
D. Hashing

354. What is the primary focus of incident response in cybersecurity?
A. Monitoring network performance
B. Preparing for and responding to security incidents
C. Developing new software applications
D. Managing financial records

355. What does business continuity planning primarily aim to achieve?
A. Recovering IT systems after a disaster
B. Ensuring the organization continues to operate during a disaster
C. Monitoring network traffic
D. Developing marketing strategies

356. What is the main goal of disaster recovery within an organization?
A. Creating new business opportunities
B. Recovering IT and information processing capabilities after a disaster
C. Developing employee training programs
D. Monitoring stock market trends

357. Which organization supports the approach where disaster recovery plans take over if incident response and business continuity plans fail?
A. ISO
B. NIST
C. (ISC)2
D. ITIL

358. What was the consequence of the UK hospital system not having a business continuity plan in 2016?
A. Increased hospital revenue
B. 3,000 medical procedures were canceled
C. Improved patient care
D. Better network security

Practice Questions

359. Which of the following is a key element of incident response governance?
A. Business development strategy
B. Marketing plan
C. Incident response policy
D. Financial audit

360. In the context of incident response, what is an 'event'?
A. A scheduled meeting
B. An occurrence of an activity on an information system
C. A company picnic
D. A stock market crash

361. What does the term 'exploit' refer to in incident response terminology?
A. A backup plan for IT systems
B. An action or tool that takes advantage of a system vulnerability
C. A scheduled software update
D. A marketing campaign

362. What is the primary purpose of an incident response plan?
A. To outline the organization's approach to incident response
B. To develop new software
C. To manage financial records
D. To increase sales

363. Which phase of the incident response process involves planning and resourcing?
A. Detection and analysis
B. Containment
C. Preparation
D. Eradication

364. What is the first step in the NIST incident response process?
A. Detection and analysis
B. Preparation

Practice Questions

C. Containment
D. Recovery

365. Which role is typically responsible for coordinating the activities of the incident response team?
A. CFO
B. CIO
C. Incident response manager or lead
D. Marketing director

366. What does 'insourcing' refer to in the context of incident response team staffing?
A. Hiring external consultants
B. Purchasing third-party services
C. Using in-house personnel for incident response
D. Outsourcing incident management entirely

367. Which of the following is considered a threat actor in incident response terminology?
A. Software update
B. Employee misbehavior
C. Hacker
D. Backup plan

368. What is the primary purpose of the detection and analysis phase?
A. To develop new security policies
B. To determine when something bad is happening
C. To train employees on incident response
D. To notify external stakeholders about incidents

369. Which of the following is not a common attack?
A. Man-in-The-Middle
B. Phishing
C. Social engineering
D. Zero Day

Practice Questions

370. What type of attack involves an attacker tricking an employee into performing a nonsecure activity?
A. Web application
B. Social engineering
C. Network
D. Misconfiguration

371. What is the role of logs in the detection and analysis phase?
A. To automate incident response
B. To capture and store events for later retrieval and analysis
C. To replace IDS/IPS systems
D. To provide real-time threat intelligence

372. Which tool aggregates and correlates event logs from various sources into a central repository?
A. IDS/IPS
B. SIEM
C. Endpoint protection
D. Threat intelligence

373. What is the purpose of incident documentation and triage?
A. To develop new security policies
B. To train employees on incident response
C. To document and track incident investigations and prioritize incidents
D. To notify external stakeholders about incidents

374. Which of the following is a key element of incident documentation?
A. Developing new policies
B. Contact information for relevant parties
C. Training employees
D. Setting up new security tools

375. Which system only/ detects and alerts personnel that an attack may be occurring without actively blocking it?

Practice Questions

A. Intrusion Prevention System (IPS)
B. Security Information and Event Management (SIEM)
C. Endpoint protection
D. Intrusion Detection System (IDS)

376. What is a common method to prevent the spread of an incident beyond the network perimeter?
A. Endpoint isolation
B. Account containment
C. Updating perimeter firewall policies
D. Disabling user accounts

377. What is the process of removing an attacker's foothold in the environment called?
A. Detection
B. Containment
C. Eradication
D. Recovery

378. Who is primarily responsible for overseeing the business continuity planning process?
A. IT Manager
B. Business Continuity Coordinator
C. Chief Financial Officer
D. Human Resources Manager

379. What is the purpose of a Business Impact Analysis (BIA)?
A. To analyze potential security threats to the organization
B. To understand business functions and determine critical ones for restoration after a disaster
C. To evaluate employee performance during a disaster
D. To identify potential new business opportunities

380. Which of the following is not typically a component of a business continuity project plan?

Practice Questions

A. Project goals and requirements
B. Employee salary reviews
C. Project schedule with milestones
D. List of deliverables and work products

381. What does MTD stand for in the context of business continuity planning?
A. Maximum Tolerable Downtime
B. Minimum Time for Disaster Recovery
C. Maximum Tolerable Disaster
D. Minimum Tolerable Downtime

382. Which department is not typically represented in a business continuity plan committee?
A. IT Department
B. Security Department
C. Marketing Department
D. Legal Department

383. In a phased approach to business continuity planning, what is the initial phase usually focused on?
A. Addressing the entire organization at once
B. Creating a plan for a portion of the organization
C. Immediate implementation of preventive controls
D. Finalizing the business continuity documentation

384. Which of the following is an example of preventive control in business continuity planning?
A. Business Impact Analysis (BIA)
B. Fortification of facilities
C. Maximum Tolerable Downtime (MTD)
D. Risk calculation

385. What should be done after obtaining management buy-in for a business continuity plan?

Practice Questions

A. Finalize the plan without further input
B. Start the recovery process immediately
C. Form a business continuity plan committee
D. Conduct employee performance reviews

386. Why is it important to place business continuity documentation under configuration control?
A. To ensure it is only accessible to senior management
B. To track changes and ensure the latest procedures are used during a disaster
C. To keep it secret from external auditors
D. To comply with employee privacy regulations

387. Which of the following steps is not part of performing a Business Impact Analysis (BIA)?
A. Identify the organization's critical business functions
B. Determine how long the functions can be without resources
C. Calculate the risk for each business function
D. Develop new marketing strategies

388. What is the purpose of the Business Impact Analysis (BIA) in BCM?
A. To develop communication plans
B. To identify the priorities, resources, minimum downtimes, and recovery times
C. To create a public relations strategy
D. To define training schedules

389. Which of the following is not a typical category addressed in recovery strategies?
A. Business process recovery
B. Facility recovery
C. Customer satisfaction recovery
D. Data recovery

390. What does RTO stand for in the context of BCM?

Practice Questions

A. Recovery Time Operation
B. Recovery Time Objective
C. Response Time Operation
D. Response Time Objective

391. Which testing method involves reviewing the business continuity plan by a group of representatives from each department?
A. Checklist testing
B. Simulation testing
C. Structured walk-through testing
D. Full-interruption testing

392. What type of site is fully-equipped and configured with up-to-date software, ready to go at a moment's notice?
A. Hot site
B. Warm site
C. Cold site
D. Tertiary site

393. What does WRT stand for in the context of BCM?
A. Work Recovery Time
B. Work Response Time
C. Written Recovery Time
D. Written Response Time

394. Which testing method involves shutting down the operational site to simulate an actual disaster?
A. Parallel testing
B. Full-interruption testing
C. Simulation testing
D. Checklist testing

395. What is the primary focus of a Disaster Recovery Plan (DRP)?
A. IT and communications functions
B. Employee safety

Practice Questions

C. Public relations
D. Supply chain recovery

396. Which of the following best describes a cold site?
A. A fully operational site with all equipment and data in place
B. A site with equipment but no data or software
C. An empty building requiring significant setup before use
D. A site used for data backup only

397. Why is it important to maintain security during the activation of a DRP?
A. To ensure encryption protocols are followed
B. To maintain confidentiality, availability, and integrity of resources
C. To meet annual compliance requirements
D. To create backup copies of all data

398. What type of network communication does a LAN enable?
A. Between continents
B. Between computing devices within limited facilities
C. Between different countries
D. Between different cities

399. What is a wireless LAN referred to as?
A. W-LAN
B. WiLAN
C. WLAN
D. W-Lan

400. Which of the following is true about LANs?
A. They cover large geographic areas
B. They are always wired
C. They cover limited geographic areas and can be wired or wireless
D. They are operated by multiple entities

401. Which of the following methods is used to ensure that data integrity and authenticity are maintained during file transmission?

Practice Questions

A. Symmetric Encryption
B. Digital Signatures
C. Hashing
D. Data Masking

402. What does the term "Advanced Persistent Threat (APT)" describe in the context of cybersecurity?
A. A type of malware that spreads rapidly through network vulnerabilities
B. A long-term, targeted attack by a highly skilled adversary aimed at stealing data or disrupting operations
C. A simple phishing attack designed to trick users into providing sensitive information
D. A vulnerability that can be easily exploited by common hacking tools

403. What is the purpose of a "Security Baseline" in an organization's IT infrastructure?
A. To define the minimum security requirements for systems and applications
B. To establish a process for handling security incidents and breaches
C. To identify and patch vulnerabilities in software applications
D. To monitor network traffic for unauthorized access attempts

404. In a cloud computing environment, what is the primary responsibility of a customer in the "Shared Responsibility Model"?
A. Managing physical security of the data center
B. Ensuring the security of the cloud provider's infrastructure
C. Securing the data, applications, and access controls that they manage
D. Handling the encryption of data at rest in the cloud provider's environment

405. What is the primary function of "Intrusion Prevention Systems (IPS)" in network security?
A. To identify and log potential security threats in real-time
B. To detect and block malicious traffic based on predefined security policies
C. To provide encryption for data transmitted over the network

Practice Questions

D. To monitor and manage user access to network resources

406. Which of the following attack vectors is specifically designed to exploit vulnerabilities in the web application layer?
A. Cross-Site Scripting (XSS)
B. SQL Injection
C. Denial of Service (DoS)
D. Man-in-the-Middle (MitM)

407. In the context of access control, what is the main purpose of "Role-Based Access Control (RBAC)"?
A. To grant access based on individual user identities and attributes
B. To restrict access based on the user's location and device
C. To assign permissions based on predefined roles within an organization
D. To enforce security policies based on user behavior and actions

408. What is the significance of "Network Segmentation" in mitigating the impact of a security breach?
A. It improves the performance of network devices by reducing traffic congestion.
B. It isolates network segments to limit the spread of an attack and protect critical systems.
C. It encrypts data transmitted between different network segments.
D. It provides redundancy to ensure network availability during a breach.

409. Which of the following methods is most effective in protecting against "Replay Attacks" in network communications?
A. Public Key Infrastructure (PKI)
B. Time-based One-Time Passwords (TOTP)
C. Digital Signatures
D. Hashing with Salts

410. In the context of a Business Continuity Plan (BCP), what is the purpose of a "Business Impact Analysis (BIA)"?
A. To identify and mitigate risks associated with business operations

Practice Questions

B. To evaluate the financial implications of potential disruptions
C. To determine the critical functions and resources necessary for business continuity
D. To develop detailed recovery procedures for IT systems

411. Which cryptographic protocol is specifically designed to secure communications over an unsecured network and provides mutual authentication between client and server?
A. Transport Layer Security (TLS)
B. Secure Hypertext Transfer Protocol (HTTPS)
C. Internet Protocol Security (IPsec)
D. Simple Object Access Protocol (SOAP)

412. In a multi-tier architecture, what is the primary function of the "Application Layer" in terms of security?
A. To manage physical network devices and connections
B. To ensure secure communication between application and database layers
C. To enforce user authentication and authorization mechanisms
D. To perform data encryption and decryption operations

413. What is the key difference between "Symmetric Key Encryption" and "Asymmetric Key Encryption"?
A. Symmetric Key Encryption uses a single key for both encryption and decryption, while Asymmetric Key Encryption uses a pair of keys.
B. Symmetric Key Encryption provides higher security than Asymmetric Key Encryption.
C. Asymmetric Key Encryption is faster and more efficient than Symmetric Key Encryption.
D. Symmetric Key Encryption is primarily used for digital signatures, while Asymmetric Key Encryption is used for data encryption.

414. What is the primary objective of "Security Information and Event Management (SIEM)" systems in an organization?
A. To prevent unauthorized access to physical assets

Practice Questions

B. To provide centralized monitoring, analysis, and response to security events and incidents
C. To manage and enforce data protection policies across the organization
D. To perform vulnerability assessments and penetration testing

415. In the context of network security, what does the term "Defense in Depth" refer to?
A. Implementing multiple layers of security controls to protect against various threats
B. Conducting regular vulnerability assessments and patch management
C. Restricting access to network resources based on user roles and permissions
D. Encrypting all network traffic to prevent unauthorized interception

416. What is the primary focus of the "Incident Response Plan (IRP)" during the initial phase of an incident?
A. To analyze the root cause of the incident
B. To contain and limit the impact of the incident
C. To communicate with external stakeholders and regulatory bodies
D. To recover and restore normal operations

417. What does the "Principle of Least Privilege" entail in an organization's security practices?
A. Granting users access to all resources needed for their role
B. Providing users with minimal permissions required to perform their duties
C. Restricting access to sensitive data to high-level executives only
D. Allowing temporary elevated privileges during emergencies

418. Which regulatory framework specifically addresses the security and privacy of healthcare information in the United States?
A. General Data Protection Regulation (GDPR)
B. Sarbanes-Oxley Act (SOX)
C. Health Insurance Portability and Accountability Act (HIPAA)
D. Federal Information Security Management Act (FISMA)

Practice Questions

Answers

1. **Answer:** B

Explanation: Cybersecurity aims to protect assets from cyber threats. It is about providing the right amount of protection to each asset based on its risks. This approach ensures that assets are protected from unauthorized access, use, disclosure, disruption, modification, or destruction. By doing so, cybersecurity helps to minimize the risk of cyber attacks.

2. **Answer:** B

Explanation: The role of security has evolved over time. In the past, security focused on physical protection, such as locks and alarms. Today, security also includes digital protection, such as firewalls and encryption, to safeguard against cyber threats. This shift recognizes that cyber threats are a major concern in today's digital age.

3. **Answer:** B

Explanation: E-mail is a function that depends on information resources. It relies on computer systems, networks, and data to operate. E-mail is a common example of how information resources are used in everyday life. It's an essential tool for communication in modern times.

4. **Answer:** B

Explanation: Cybersecurity has a dual nature, like a coin with two sides. One side is about protecting against cyber threats, while the other side is about ensuring the confidentiality, integrity, and availability of information resources. This dual nature highlights the importance of balancing protection with access and use. By doing so, cybersecurity ensures that information resources are both secure and usable.

Answers

5. **Answer:** B.

Explanation: Information resources require protection because they are vulnerable to attacks. Cyber threats, such as hacking and malware, can compromise the security of information resources. If left unprotected, information resources can be stolen, damaged, or destroyed. By protecting information resources, cybersecurity helps to prevent these types of attacks.

6. **Answer:** B

Explanation: Robust cybersecurity measures are essential for protecting information resources. These measures include firewalls, encryption, access control, and more. By implementing robust cybersecurity measures, organizations can help prevent cyber attacks and protect their information resources. This is especially important in today's digital age.

7. **Answer:** C

Explanation: The "need to know" principle restricts access to information or resources to only those individuals who require it to perform their duties, enhancing security by minimizing unnecessary exposure.

8. **Answer:** B

Explanation: The concept of "need to know" relies on authentication to verify a user's identity. By verifying identity, authentication ensures that users only have access to information resources that they need to perform their tasks. This helps to prevent unauthorized access and cyber attacks.

9. **Answer:** C

Explanation: Authentication does not encrypt data. Encryption is a separate cybersecurity measure that protects data by making it unreadable

Answers

to unauthorized individuals. While authentication verifies identity, encryption protects data in transit or at rest.

10. **Answer:** B

Explanation: The process of authentication helps to verify the user's identity. By doing so, authentication ensures that only authorized individuals have access to information resources. This helps to prevent unauthorized access and cyber attacks.

11. **Answer:** B

Explanation: Cyber criminals typically aim to achieve financial gain or disrupt operations when they attack information systems. This can involve stealing valuable assets such as money, intellectual property, or personal data or causing disruptions that impact business continuity and reputation.

12. **Answer:** C

Explanation: Cyber criminals are primarily interested in assets that can provide financial gain or strategic advantage. This includes stealing money through fraudulent transactions or intellectual property such as trade secrets, proprietary software, or research data that can be sold or exploited.

13. **Answer:** D

Explanation: Cyber criminals can be motivated by personal gain (e.g., financial profit), financial gain (e.g., stealing money or valuable assets), or political gain (e.g., espionage or sabotage), depending on their objectives and affiliations.

14. **Answer:** C

Explanation: Cyber criminals target a wide range of organizations that own and operate information systems, including businesses of all sizes,

Answers

government agencies, educational institutions, and healthcare providers, due to their valuable data and resources.

15. **Answer:** B

Explanation: A cyber criminal's attack can disrupt the normal operation of an information system, leading to downtime, loss of productivity, and potentially significant financial losses. This disruption can also affect customer trust and damage the organization's reputation.

16. **Answer:** C

Explanation: Cyber criminals do not aim to enhance system security; instead, they seek to exploit weaknesses in security defenses to achieve their malicious objectives, such as stealing information, disrupting operations, or causing damage.

17. **Answer:** B

Explanation: Offensive attacks refer to cyber criminals actively targeting and exploiting vulnerabilities in systems to compromise or gain unauthorized access to sensitive information, disrupt operations, or achieve other malicious goals.

18. **Answer:** D

Explanation: Charitable gain, or motives related to philanthropy or altruism, is not a typical motivation for cyber criminal activities. Motives typically revolve around personal gain, financial profit, political influence, or malicious intent.

19. **Answer:** D

Explanation: Cyber criminals might target the Information Technology sector specifically for intellectual property theft due to the valuable

Answers

technologies, innovations, and software developments that can be stolen, reverse-engineered, or sold for profit.

20. **Answer:** C

Explanation: The relationship between cyber criminals and the organizations they attack is typically adversarial. Cyber criminals are attackers seeking to exploit vulnerabilities in the target organization's systems and networks, which are the targets of their malicious activities.

21. **Answer:** B

Explanation: The primary goal of cybersecurity professionals engaged in cyber defense is to protect organizations from cyberattacks by implementing preventive measures, detecting threats early, responding swiftly to incidents, and recovering effectively to minimize impact.

22. **Answer:** D

Explanation: Cybersecurity professionals focus on protecting systems and data from cyberattacks, detecting threats, and responding to and recovering from cyber incidents. They do not typically develop new hardware for organizations, as this is the role of hardware engineers. Instead, cybersecurity experts may collaborate with hardware teams to ensure security features are incorporated, but their primary responsibilities lie in defense, detection, and incident response.

23. **Answer:** B

Explanation: Detecting cyberattacks is a key part of defensive strategies, as it involves monitoring systems and networks to identify and respond to threats in order to protect the organization's assets.

24. **Answer:** B

Answers

Explanation: Cybersecurity professionals are primarily responsible for defending systems, networks, and data from cyber threats. Their role revolves around implementing protective measures, monitoring potential attacks, and responding to incidents to safeguard organizational assets.

25. **Answer:** B

Explanation: When a cyber incident occurs, cybersecurity professionals respond by executing incident response plans to mitigate the impact, investigate the incident, contain the threat, and recover affected systems and data. Their goal is to minimize damage and restore normal operations as quickly as possible.

26. **Answer:** C

Explanation: Detecting cyberattacks is crucial for identifying and mitigating threats in real-time. The primary objective is to prevent further damage, protect sensitive data, and ensure the security of systems by responding promptly and effectively to any detected threats.

27. **Answer:** B

Explanation: The primary focus of cyber defense is to protect the organization as a whole, encompassing its people, processes, technology, data, and reputation from a wide range of cyber threats and attacks.

28. **Answer:** D

Explanation: Developing marketing strategies is not part of the cyber defense process. Cyber defense involves activities such as risk assessment, threat detection, vulnerability management, incident response, and continuous improvement of security measures.

29. **Answer:** A

Answers

Explanation: The three core types of protection in cybersecurity are often referred to as the CIA triad: Confidentiality (ensuring data is accessible only to authorized parties), Integrity (ensuring data is accurate and trustworthy), and Availability (ensuring data and systems are accessible when needed). These principles guide cybersecurity practices to protect information and systems effectively.

30. **Answer:** D

Explanation: Authentication verifies the identity of users or systems and is crucial for access control, but it is not part of the CIA triad, which focuses on Confidentiality, Availability, and Integrity of data.

31. **Answer:** B

Explanation: Integrity ensures that data remains accurate and consistent throughout its lifecycle, protecting it from unauthorized modification or corruption.

32. **Answer:** C

Explanation: Understanding Confidentiality, Availability, and Integrity helps professionals implement appropriate security measures to safeguard data against threats.

33. **Answer:** C

Explanation: Integrity in the CIA triad refers to ensuring that data remains accurate, complete, and unaltered throughout its lifecycle, maintaining its reliability and trustworthiness.

34. **Answer:** C

Answers

Explanation: Cyber criminals compromise confidentiality by gaining unauthorized access to sensitive data, thereby bypassing security measures intended to restrict access to authorized individuals only.

35. **Answer:** C

Explanation: Access controls help protect data against breaches of confidentiality by ensuring that only authorized individuals or systems have access to sensitive information. This helps prevent unauthorized access and disclosure of data.

36. **Answer:** B

Explanation: Access controls are used in cybersecurity to enforce policies and procedures that restrict access to data, systems, and networks to authorized users only, thereby protecting against unauthorized access and ensuring data confidentiality and integrity.

37. **Answer:** A

Explanation: Cryptography ensures confidentiality by encrypting data, making it unreadable to unauthorized persons who do not possess the decryption keys. This prevents unauthorized access and protects sensitive information from being compromised.

38. **Answer:** C

Explanation: Cryptography protects the confidentiality of data both when it is stored (data at rest) and when it is transmitted over networks (data in transit), ensuring that sensitive information remains secure and private.

39. **Answer:** C

Answers

Explanation: Data at rest refers to inactive data stored in databases, file systems, or other storage media where it is not actively being accessed or transmitted.

40. **Answer:** C

Explanation: A cryptographic key is what enables a cryptographic algorithm to perform its function. It is used to encrypt plaintext into ciphertext and decrypt ciphertext back into plaintext. The key is crucial for ensuring the security and confidentiality of data in cryptographic operations.

41. **Answer:** C

Explanation: Confidentiality ensures that information is accessible only to those who are authorized to view it, protecting it from unauthorized access. This is a core principle of the CIA triad, which is central to information security.

42. **Answer:** C

Explanation: Integrity in electronically signed contracts is crucial to ensure that the data remains unaltered and authentic after the contract has been signed. This means that the contract's content cannot be changed by unauthorized parties, preserving the document's original intent and terms.

43. **Answer:** B

Explanation: Ensuring data integrity guarantees that information remains unchanged and trustworthy, preventing unauthorized alterations that could compromise its accuracy.

44. **Answer:** C

Answers

Explanation: Firewalls are designed to prevent unauthorized access to or from a private network. They filter incoming and outgoing traffic based on security rules to protect network resources from external threats.

45. **Answer:** B

Explanation: Threat actors are individuals or groups who pose a threat to information security by attempting to exploit vulnerabilities, gain unauthorized access, or disrupt systems for malicious purposes.

46. **Answer:** B

Explanation: Security controls aim to protect the CIA triad, ensuring data remains confidential, accurate, and available to authorized users while defending against threats.

47. **Answer:** B

Explanation: Authorization requires verifying the identity of users to determine their permissions and access rights, ensuring they only interact with resources appropriate to their role.

48. **Answer:** B

Explanation: To prevent unauthorized access and threats - Protecting information assets safeguards data integrity, confidentiality, and availability, mitigating risks associated with unauthorized access, breaches, or data loss.

49. **Answer:** B

Explanation: Countermeasures are proactive measures or controls implemented to mitigate risks, defend against threats, and enhance the security posture of information systems.

Answers

50. **Answer:** B

Explanation: Threat actors, such as hackers or insiders, target information assets to exploit vulnerabilities, gain unauthorized access, or disrupt operations, posing risks to data security.

51. **Answer:** C

Explanation: The principle of Least Privilege ensures that users have only the permissions they need to perform their job functions. This reduces the risk of accidental or intentional misuse of access.

52. **Answer:** B

Explanation: Business Continuity Planning (BCP) focuses on maintaining essential functions and minimizing disruption during unexpected events, such as natural disasters or cyberattacks, to ensure that business operations can continue.

53. **Answer:** B

Explanation: Authentication validates the identity of users through credentials or authentication factors, ensuring secure access to systems and data while preventing unauthorized entry.

54. **Answer:** C

Explanation: If authentication fails, users are denied access to the system or resource they are trying to log into, safeguarding against unauthorized entry and potential security breaches.

55. **Answer:** A

Answers

Explanation: Logging in involves users entering their credentials (username/password) or using authentication factors to access the system, initiating the authentication process to verify their identity securely.

56. **Answer:** B

Explanation: During registration, users typically agree to the terms of service, which outline the rules and conditions for using the platform or service, ensuring compliance and security.

57. **Answer:** B

Explanation: Organizations may require users to provide identification cards to verify their identity during the registration process, enhancing security and ensuring that only authorized individuals gain access.

58. **Answer:** B

Explanation: Verification factors like passwords or biometrics are used whenever users log in to verify their identity and ensure secure access to systems or resources, protecting against unauthorized activities.

59. **Answer:** C

Explanation Registration establishes user profiles within the authentication system, assigning credentials and capturing necessary information to manage and authenticate user identities effectively.

60. **Answer:** B

Explanation: Authentication is part of user management, which includes managing user identities, permissions, and access controls to ensure secure interactions with systems and protect against unauthorized access.

Answers

61. Answer: B

Explanation: Security measures need to be customized to fit the unique requirements, risks, and contexts of different environments. This approach ensures that security controls are appropriate and effective, addressing specific threats and vulnerabilities while aligning with the organization's objectives and regulatory requirements. Tailoring security efforts also allows for efficient resource allocation and adaptability to changing circumstances.

62. Answer: B

Explanation: The ultimate goal of authentication is to verify users' identities and allow appropriate access to systems and resources based on their credentials, ensuring secure and authorized usage.

63. Answer: B

Explanation: Authenticity in information security ensures that data transmissions are legitimate and have not been altered or compromised during transmission, maintaining data integrity.

64. Answer: A

Explanation: Nonrepudiation guarantees that the sender cannot deny sending a message or data, providing proof of origin and ensuring accountability in communication.

65. Answer: C

Explanation: Authenticity and nonrepudiation are vital in data transmission to verify the legitimacy and trustworthiness of data and the transmission process, which is crucial for maintaining security and reliability.

66. Answer: C

Answers

Explanation: Authenticity and nonrepudiation are achieved through specific processes and technologies that validate the sender's identity and ensure message integrity, which is essential for secure communication.

67. **Answer:** D

Explanation: Nonrepudiation is a security principle that ensures a party in a communication cannot deny the authenticity of their signature on a document or a message that they originated.

68. **Answer:** C

Explanation: Users trust data and transmission processes by verifying authenticity (provenance) and nonrepudiation (accountability), ensuring reliable and trustworthy communication.

69. **Answer:** B

Explanation: Security Operations encompasses the continuous monitoring of IT environments to detect and respond to security incidents. This includes managing security alerts, handling breaches, and ensuring overall security posture.

70. **Answer:** C

Explanation: Nonrepudiation ensures that the sender cannot deny sending data, which is crucial for establishing trust and accountability in communication.

71. **Answer:** B

Explanation: During the 'Identify Targets' phase, attackers aim to identify an organization's critical information assets and vulnerabilities, essential for planning effective attacks.

Answers

72. Answer: B

Explanation: Attackers use automated tools to generate lists of target computer systems within a network, facilitating systematic probing and potential exploitation.

73. Answer: B

Explanation: Probing further after identifying target systems aims to uncover vulnerabilities that can be exploited to gain unauthorized access, a critical step in cyber attacks.

74. Answer: D

Explanation: Weather patterns are not targets typically identified by attackers, distinguishing them from conventional information assets or vulnerabilities.

75. Answer: B

Explanation: Attackers seek to exploit vulnerabilities found within an organization's information assets to gain unauthorized access or cause disruption, compromising security.

76. Answer: C

Explanation: Attackers often create or use specialized tools to aid in their attacks. These tools can range from simple scripts to sophisticated software designed to exploit vulnerabilities, gain unauthorized access, or disrupt systems. Having the right tools can significantly enhance the effectiveness and scope of cyberattacks.

77. Answer: D

Answers

Explanation: Attack phases generally do not involve notifying the enterprise, focusing instead on covertly gaining unauthorized access and avoiding detection.

78. **Answer:** A

Explanation: Internal drivers for a security program include meeting compliance requirements and ensuring adherence to regulatory standards for security.

79. **Answer:** B

Explanation: Security programs are managed through subprograms or functions tailored to address specific security needs and objectives within an organization.

80. **Answer:** B

Explanation: Subprograms within a security program manage cybersecurity based on organizational requirements and priorities, optimizing security measures.

81. **Answer:** B

Explanation: Security program activities are documented and managed through established policies, procedures, and internal standards to ensure consistency and compliance.

82. **Answer:** C

Explanation: Internal standards within a security program include organizational procedures defining how security measures are implemented and maintained.

Answers

83. Answer: B

Explanation: Staffing a security program involves ensuring effective security governance and management to oversee and implement security measures.

84. Answer: B

Explanation: Policies, procedures, and internal standards collectively document and guide security activities within an organization, ensuring clarity and consistency.

85. Answer: B

Explanation: The selection and implementation of security controls are based on security governance and risk management assessments to mitigate identified risks effectively.

86. Answer: D

Explanation: Security controls protect an organization's valuable information assets from various threats and vulnerabilities, ensuring confidentiality, integrity, and availability.

87. Answer: C

Explanation: Security governance guides the selection and implementation of appropriate security controls to mitigate identified risks effectively, enhancing overall security posture.

88. Answer: B

Explanation: Implementing security controls is a response to risk assessments and governance outcomes, addressing identified risks to enhance organizational security.

Answers

89. **Answer:** C

Explanation: The selection of security controls should be based on structured risk analysis, not personal opinions or historical sales data, ensuring effective risk mitigation.

90. **Answer:** C

Explanation: Although profit maximization, professional ethics, and market expansion are significant, the primary focus of an organization's activities is usually on customer satisfaction. By prioritizing customer satisfaction, organizations aim to build strong relationships, encourage repeat business, and ultimately drive growth and success.

91. **Answer:** C

Explanation: The ethical approach of an organization involves making decisions and taking actions that are morally right and ethically sound beyond mere legal compliance.

92. **Answer:** C

Explanation: Market share growth is correct because organizations typically prioritize ethical guidelines, professional ethics, and moral correctness over market expansion. While growing market share is important, it is secondary to maintaining ethical and moral standards.

93. **Answer:** B

Explanation: Ensuring ethical practices within an organization is achieved through corporate policies that define expected behavior and ethical standards, promoting integrity and accountability.

Answers

94. **Answer:** B

Explanation: Commitment to ethical standards implies prioritizing actions and decisions that uphold moral principles and contribute positively to stakeholders and society.

95. **Answer:** C

Explanation: Ethical guidelines in an organization are part of corporate governance practices that guide how the organization operates and makes decisions, aligning with ethical standards.

96. **Answer:** D

Explanation: Risk management involves identifying and managing vulnerabilities, threats, and risks to protect organizational assets and investments from potential harm and losses.

97. **Answer:** B

Explanation: Organizations implement security controls to defend their assets against various risks, including cyber threats and vulnerabilities, enhancing overall security posture.

98. **Answer:** A

Explanation: Effective risk management oversight involves establishing a risk oversight board to monitor and manage organizational risks proactively, ensuring comprehensive risk mitigation strategies.

99. **Answer:** A

Explanation: Besides the Chief Risk Officer (CRO) or Chief Financial Officer (CFO), the Chief Information Security Officer (CISO) plays a critical role in overseeing risk management within organizations.

Answers

100. **Answer:** C

Explanation: The Zero Trust model operates on the principle of "never trust, always verify." It requires verification for every request and does not automatically trust internal network traffic, thereby minimizing the risk of insider threats and unauthorized access.

101. **Answer:** C

Explanation: Access control mechanisms ensure that only individuals with proper authorization can access resources or enter secure areas within an organization. By managing who can access what, organizations prevent unauthorized entry, protect sensitive information, and maintain overall security integrity.

102. **Answer:** B

Explanation: The principle of least privilege dictates that users should be granted the minimum permissions necessary to perform their job functions. This approach reduces the risk of unauthorized access or accidental misuse of sensitive data, enhancing overall security posture by limiting exposure to critical assets.

103. **Answer:** C

Explanation: Segregation of Duties (SoD) is a foundational principle in internal controls, where tasks are divided among different individuals to prevent any single person from having complete control over a process. This separation enhances accountability, reduces the likelihood of errors, and mitigates the risk of fraud by requiring collusion between multiple parties for malicious activities to occur.

104. **Answer:** B

Answers

Explanation: The two-person rule mandates that certain critical actions or decisions must involve the participation of at least two authorized individuals. This practice adds an additional layer of security by ensuring that no single person can execute sensitive operations independently, thereby reducing the risk of errors, fraud, or unauthorized actions that could compromise organizational security or integrity.

105. **Answer:** B

Explanation: Authentication based on "something you know" involves verifying a user's identity using knowledge-based credentials such as passwords, PINs, or answers to security questions. This method ensures that only individuals who possess the correct credentials can gain access to systems or sensitive information, safeguarding against unauthorized access and protecting user accounts from malicious activities like unauthorized logins or data breaches.

106. **Answer:** A

Explanation: Identification in access control is the initial process of presenting identifying information, such as a username or ID, to the system. This step establishes the user's identity and initiates the authentication process to verify that the user is who they claim to be, ensuring that access rights can be accurately determined and enforced based on their identity.

107. **Answer:** B

Explanation: Authentication in access control involves verifying the validity of the credentials presented during the identification phase to ensure that the user is indeed who they claim to be. This verification process typically includes validating passwords, biometric data, security tokens, or other authentication factors to grant or deny access to systems, applications, or resources based on the user's authenticated identity.

Answers

108. **Answer:** C

Explanation: Authorization in access control determines what actions or resources a properly authenticated user is permitted to access based on their role, permissions, or other attributes. This process ensures that users have appropriate access privileges aligned with their job responsibilities while preventing unauthorized access to sensitive data or critical systems, thereby maintaining security and compliance with organizational policies.

109. **Answer:** C

Explanation: Accountability in access control involves logging and monitoring user activities, including login attempts, access requests, and operations performed on systems or data. These activity logs provide a detailed audit trail that enables organizations to trace actions back to specific users, detect suspicious or unauthorized behavior, and ensure accountability for compliance with security policies and regulatory requirements.

110. **Answer:** A

Explanation: Password rotation is a security best practice that involves periodically changing passwords to mitigate the risk of compromised credentials. By requiring users to update their passwords at regular intervals, organizations reduce the likelihood of unauthorized access due to password theft, guessing, or other forms of credential compromise, thereby enhancing overall system security and protecting sensitive data from unauthorized disclosure or misuse.

111. **Answer:** B

Explanation: Privileged Access Management (PAM) focuses on controlling and monitoring access to privileged accounts, which have elevated permissions and pose a higher risk if compromised. By implementing strict controls, monitoring activities, and limiting the use of privileged accounts to authorized personnel and specific tasks, organizations can mitigate the

Answers

risk of insider threats, unauthorized access, and malicious activities that could compromise system integrity and data security.

112. Answer: B

Explanation: Privileged accounts have elevated permissions that grant users access to critical systems, sensitive data, or administrative functions within an organization. Due to their heightened access rights, these accounts are highly coveted targets for attackers seeking to exploit vulnerabilities, escalate privileges, or conduct malicious activities. Effective management and security controls are essential to safeguard privileged accounts and prevent unauthorized access that could lead to data breaches, financial losses, or operational disruptions.

113. Answer: A

Explanation: The Principle of Least Privilege (PoLP) is a security guideline that recommends restricting user permissions to only those necessary to perform their job functions. By minimizing access rights to the minimum required for legitimate tasks, PoLP reduces the potential impact of compromised accounts or insider threats, limits exposure to sensitive information, and strengthens overall security posture by enforcing strict access controls based on least privilege principles.

114. Answer: B

Explanation: Limiting the number of privileged accounts within an organization is crucial for reducing the attack surface and minimizing the risk of unauthorized access or misuse of critical systems. By consolidating and closely managing privileged accounts, organizations can improve security posture, streamline access management processes, and enhance oversight to prevent potential security breaches or insider threats associated with excessive account privileges.

Answers

115. Answer: B

Explanation: Privileged Access Management (PAM) systems securely store and manage credentials, such as passwords, SSH keys, or API tokens, used to access privileged accounts. By centralizing credential management and enforcing strict access controls, PAM solutions help prevent unauthorized access, reduce the risk of credential theft or misuse, and ensure accountability for privileged activities performed within IT environments.

116. Answer: A

Explanation: Residual risk is the level of risk that remains after implementing all mitigation strategies and controls. It represents a risk that cannot be fully eliminated and must be managed or accepted.

117. Answer: D

Explanation: Security controls encompass administrative, logical, and technical measures designed to protect information systems, data, and resources from security threats and vulnerabilities. Administrative controls involve policies, procedures, and guidelines that govern security practices and user behavior. Logical controls implement access restrictions and encryption to protect data integrity and confidentiality. Technical controls use technology-based solutions such as firewalls, antivirus software, and intrusion detection systems to monitor, detect, and respond to security incidents.

118. Answer: C

Explanation: Firewalls are network security devices that monitor and control incoming and outgoing traffic based on predetermined security rules. By filtering network traffic and enforcing access policies, firewalls help prevent unauthorized access, block malicious content, and protect against cyber threats such as malware, denial-of-service attacks, and unauthorized access attempts. Deploying firewalls as part of a comprehensive security

Answers

strategy enhances network security posture and reduces the risk of data breaches or compromise of sensitive information.

119. **Answer:** B

Explanation: Logical access control mechanisms regulate user access to systems, applications, or data based on their authenticated identity and authorized permissions. By enforcing access policies and authentication protocols, these controls ensure that only authorized users can access specific resources or perform allowed actions, thereby protecting sensitive information, maintaining data confidentiality, and preventing unauthorized use or manipulation of IT assets.

120. **Answer:** C

Explanation: Access control models define methodologies for managing and enforcing access rights based on user attributes, roles, or ownership of resources. Discretionary Access Control (DAC) grants users discretion over their resources. Attribute-Based Access Control (ABAC) evaluates access decisions based on attributes associated with users, resources, and environmental conditions. Role-Based Access Control (RBAC) assigns permissions based on predefined roles that reflect job responsibilities, simplifying access management and ensuring compliance with security policies and regulatory requirements.

121. **Answer:** A

Explanation: DAC allows users to control access permissions to their resources, granting them discretion over who can access their data or files. Users can set access rights for specific files or directories, determining which individuals or groups have permission to view, modify, or delete their data. DAC is commonly used in personal computing environments and collaborative settings where users require flexibility in managing access to their files or resources.

Answers

122. **Answer:** B

Explanation: In Discretionary Access Control (DAC), the owner of a resource retains control over access permissions and is responsible for setting or modifying access rights for the resource. The owner can specify which users or groups have permission to access the resource and define the level of access granted, such as read-only, write, or full control. By assigning ownership and control to the resource creator or designated user, DAC allows for decentralized access management while enabling accountability and flexibility in resource sharing.

123. **Answer:** A

Explanation: An access control matrix is a structured representation of access permissions that define which subjects (users or processes) have access to which objects (files or resources) and specifies the actions (permissions) they are allowed to perform. Each entry in the matrix corresponds to a specific combination of subject, object, and permission, facilitating centralized management of access control policies and ensuring that access rights align with organizational security requirements and data protection policies.

124. **Answer:** A

Explanation: Mandatory Access Control (MAC) is a security model commonly used in government, military, and high-security environments to enforce strict access control policies based on hierarchical security classifications. MAC mandates that access decisions are determined by system administrators or security administrators rather than by resource owners or users, ensuring that access permissions are centrally managed and strictly enforced according to predefined security policies and clearance levels.

125. **Answer:** A

Answers

Explanation: Data classification in Mandatory Access Control (MAC) categorizes information based on sensitivity levels, assigning security labels or classifications that dictate the level of protection and access controls required for each category.

126. **Answer:** A

Explanation: RBAC assigns permissions based on user roles, simplifying access management and enhancing security by ensuring users only access what is necessary for their roles.

127. **Answer:** A

Explanation: Role-Based Access Control (RBAC) provides the benefit of customizing and managing permissions based on user roles within an organization. This approach ensures that individuals have access only to the resources and information necessary for their specific roles, enhancing security and operational efficiency.

128. **Answer:** A

Explanation: ABAC, also known as policy-based or claims-based access control, dynamically determines access based on attributes like user roles, time, location, and other contextual factors.

129. **Answer:** C

Explanation: Preventive controls are designed to stop security incidents before they occur. They include measures such as firewalls, access controls, and security policies that prevent unauthorized access or malicious activity.

130. **Answer:** A

Explanation: Technologies like directories, Single Sign-On (SSO), and Federated Identity Management (FIM) manage user identities and access

Answers

across systems, enhancing security and user experience across organizational boundaries.

131. **Answer:** B

Explanation: Directories in large organizations manage logical access by organizing and providing access to user accounts and resources based on defined policies and permissions.

132. **Answer:** C

Explanation: SSO allows users to authenticate once and access multiple applications or systems without re-authenticating, enhancing user convenience and security.

133. **Answer:** A

Explanation: FIM enables organizations to establish trust relationships to use identities and credentials across multiple domains or organizations, facilitating seamless and secure collaboration.

134. **Answer:** B

Explanation: Account audits ensure regular review of both privileged/administrator and standard user accounts to enforce security policies and best practices, mitigating risks associated with unauthorized access.

135. **Answer:** B

Explanation: Logical access logs are used to detect unauthorized access or other security incidents by monitoring and reviewing access events across computers, networks, and applications.

Answers

136. **Answer:** B

Explanation: Monitoring tools provide automated alerting and review of access logs and events, enabling proactive detection and response to potential security threats in real-time.

137. **Answer:** B

Explanation: Physical access controls prevent and monitor physical attacks such as unauthorized entry, theft, and other threats by securing physical entry points to facilities.

138. **Answer:** A

Explanation: These measures secure facilities by strategically placing physical barriers like fencing and walls to control and restrict logical access through approved entry points.

139. **Answer:** B

Explanation: Bollards are used in physical access control to prevent vehicles from entering restricted areas or to minimize the risk of unauthorized vehicle access. They act as physical barriers that help protect buildings and sensitive areas from vehicular intrusion or accidents.

140. **Answer:** A

Explanation: Fencing and walls restrict access to physical areas and funnel entry through controlled points, improving physical security by preventing unauthorized access.

141. **Answer:** B

Answers

Explanation: These control physical access points by allowing one person to pass through at a time, enhancing security by regulating entry into restricted areas.

142. **Answer:** A

Explanation: A mantrap is an access control mechanism with two unlocked doors that must be passed sequentially to control and monitor entry into secure areas, enhancing physical security.

143. **Answer:** A

Explanation: Protecting the safety of facilities and assets is the primary goal of physical access control, ensuring the security and integrity of physical spaces and resources.

144. **Answer:** C

Explanation: Fail-secure doors remain locked during a disaster or system failure, maintaining security by preventing unauthorized access even in emergency situations.

145. **Answer:** C

Explanation: Black hat hackers use their skills to exploit vulnerabilities for malicious purposes, such as stealing data or disrupting services. They operate without authorization and often have malicious intent.

146. **Answer:** A

Explanation: Badge systems validate identities and grant authorized access to facilities based on assigned permissions, enhancing physical security by restricting entry to authorized personnel.

Answers

147. Answer: A

Explanation: Biometrics authenticate individuals based on unique physical characteristics like fingerprints or retina patterns to grant secure and convenient access to facilities, enhancing security by ensuring only authorized personnel enter.

148. Answer: D

Explanation: Access control models manage and enforce rules governing how users interact with system resources, ensuring secure and compliant access based on defined policies and permissions.

149. Answer: B

Explanation: Public Key Infrastructure (PKI) is used to manage digital certificates and encryption keys, enabling secure communications and verifying the identity of entities in digital transactions.

150. Answer: C

Explanation: SoD separates responsibilities among multiple individuals to prevent fraud or errors by ensuring no single person has complete control over critical tasks, enhancing accountability and security.

151. Answer: B

Explanation: Data masking involves obfuscating sensitive data to prevent unauthorized access while retaining its usability for development or testing purposes. It ensures that sensitive information is not exposed in non-production environments.

152. Answer: C

Answers

Explanation: SoD helps prevent fraud by restricting employees' access so that no one person can perform and conceal fraudulent activities without collaboration.

153. **Answer:** B

Explanation: This example ensures that the person authorizing payments (signing checks) is different from the person preparing them (writing checks), which is a classic application of SoD in financial controls.

154. **Answer:** A

Explanation: SoD is typically implemented when structuring job roles and responsibilities to ensure accountability and reduce risks associated with conflicts of interest.

155. **Answer:** A

Explanation: SoD policies usually apply to job functions that, when combined, could lead to conflicts of interest, fraud, or errors due to lack of oversight.

156. **Answer:** C

Explanation: Segregation of Duties is a fundamental internal control designed to prevent errors and fraud by ensuring that no single individual has control over all aspects of any critical function or process. By separating responsibilities, it reduces the risk of intentional manipulation or accidental errors.

157. **Answer:** C

Explanation: If one person controls both the creation and approval of financial transactions, there is an increased risk of unauthorized or inappropriate transactions.

Answers

158. **Answer:** C

Explanation: Segregation of Duties (SoD) is implemented to reduce the risk of fraud, errors, or misuse by ensuring that no single individual has control over all aspects of a critical process. By dividing responsibilities among different individuals, organizations can create checks and balances that help protect against malicious actions and inadvertent errors.

159. **Answer:** B

Explanation: Segregation of Duties (SoD) is a fundamental internal control mechanism designed to prevent fraud, errors, and abuse by ensuring that no single individual is responsible for all aspects of a transaction or process. It is a key component of an organization's overall internal control system.

160. **Answer:** B

Explanation: The two-person rule ensures that critical actions require the involvement of at least two authorized individuals, thereby increasing oversight and reducing the risk of misconduct.

161. **Answer:** C

Explanation: The NSA implemented the two-person rule in response to security breaches involving Edward Snowden to increase oversight and prevent unauthorized data access.

162. **Answer:** B

Explanation: The two-person rule is used in nuclear weapons controls to ensure that no single individual has the authority to make decisions or take actions related to the handling, deployment, or use of nuclear weapons without the verification or presence of another authorized person. This rule helps enhance security and prevent unauthorized or accidental actions.

Copyright © 2024 VERSAtile Reads. All rights reserved.
This material is protected by copyright, any infringement will be dealt with legal and punitive action.

Answers

163. **Answer:** B

Explanation: In storage areas, the two-person rule typically involves physical controls like locks that require the presence of two authorized individuals to open, ensuring security.

164. **Answer:** C

Explanation: The two-person rule is similar to the Segregation of Duties (SoD) in that both concepts are designed to enhance security and reduce the risk of unauthorized actions or errors. Both involve separating responsibilities among different individuals to create checks and balances, ensuring that no single person has complete control over critical processes.

165. **Answer:** B

Explanation: Industries requiring heightened security, such as handling sensitive materials or equipment, commonly implement the two-person rule.

166. **Answer:** A

Explanation: Edward Snowden was a government contractor working for the National Security Agency (NSA). His actions, including the unauthorized disclosure of classified information, led to increased security measures such as the two-person rule to enhance oversight and prevent similar breaches in the future.

167. **Answer:** C

Explanation: The two-person rule requires two authorized individuals to collaborate simultaneously on certain functions to ensure oversight and security.

Answers

168. **Answer:** B

Explanation: "In tandem" in the context of the two-person rule means that two individuals must work together at the same time to perform a specific task.

169. **Answer:** B

Explanation: Organizations adopt the two-person rule to enhance security by requiring collaborative verification for critical actions, reducing the risk of unauthorized activities.

170. **Answer:** B

Explanation: Network segmentation involves dividing a network into smaller segments or zones to contain and limit the impact of security breaches. It enhances security by restricting the movement of attackers and reducing the potential for widespread damage.

171. **Answer:** C

Explanation: A password is a classic example of a memorized secret used for authentication, requiring users to input specific characters to access systems or accounts.

172. **Answer:** B

Explanation: Memorized secrets, such as passwords or passphrases, are used to authenticate a user. They verify the identity of the user by requiring them to provide a secret that only they should know.

173. **Answer:** C

Explanation: Passwords can consist of a combination of numbers, letters (both uppercase and lowercase), and special characters. This diversity

Answers

enhances the complexity and security of the password, making it more resistant to being guessed or cracked.

174. **Answer:** B

Explanation: Lock combinations typically consist of alphanumeric characters and symbols, allowing for a wide range of possible combinations for security purposes.

175. **Answer:** B

Explanation: The memorized secret, such as a password or passphrase, is known only by the user who created it. It is intended to be kept confidential to ensure secure authentication and access to systems or information.

176. **Answer:** A

Explanation: Authentication through memorized secrets requires users to correctly input their password or code to verify their identity and gain access.

177. **Answer:** B

Explanation: Data masking replaces sensitive data with fictional or scrambled data that retains its format and usability, making it ideal for development and testing environments. Unlike encryption, which protects data in transit or at rest, masking is specifically designed to obscure sensitive information while preserving its functional use.

178. **Answer:** C

Explanation: A security token, unlike a memorized secret, is a physical device used to generate secure authentication codes or provide access credentials.

Answers

179. **Answer:** B

Explanation: The correct entry of a password or combination is used to verify the user's identity. This authentication process ensures that only authorized individuals can access systems, applications, or data.

180. **Answer:** B

Explanation: These are the two fundamental types of computer networks, with LANs typically confined to a single geographical location and WANs spanning larger areas or multiple locations.

181. **Answer:** C

Explanation: Ethernet, a widely used technology for Local Area Networks (LANs), is defined by the IEEE 802.3 standard. This standard specifies the physical and data link layers of Ethernet networks, including details like frame format, Media Access Control (MAC), and signaling.

182. **Answer:** B

Explanation: A MAC (Media Access Control) address is a unique identifier assigned to network interfaces for communications at the data link layer of a network segment. Its primary purpose is to uniquely identify each device connected to a network, enabling devices to communicate within the same LAN segment.

183. **Answer:** B

Explanation: SSID (Service Set Identifier) refers to the name of a wireless network that wireless devices used to identify and connect to a specific wireless LAN. It distinguishes one WLAN from another within the same area.

Copyright © 2024 VERSAtile Reads. All rights reserved.
This material is protected by copyright, any infringement will be dealt with legal and punitive action.

Answers

184. **Answer:** B

Explanation: MAC addresses operate at Layer 2, known as the Data Link Layer, in the OSI (Open Systems Interconnection) model. This layer is responsible for the reliable transmission of data frames across a physical link, and MAC addresses are used to uniquely identify devices within the same LAN.

185. **Answer:** B

Explanation: Static IP addresses are manually assigned to a device and remain fixed, providing a consistent address for services like web hosting or remote access. Dynamic IP addresses, on the other hand, are assigned automatically by a DHCP (Dynamic Host Configuration Protocol) server whenever a device connects to the network. Dynamic IPs are more common in home and office networks where devices frequently join and leave the network.

186. **Answer:** B

Explanation: Routers are networking devices that forward data packets between different computer networks, acting as gateways between networks using different protocols or addressing schemes. They determine the best path for data to travel based on network conditions, traffic load, and routing tables, enabling communication between devices on different LANs or WANs.

187. **Answer:** C

Explanation: Switches are network devices that operate at Layer 2 of the OSI model and are used to connect devices within the same LAN. They learn the MAC addresses of connected devices and use this information to intelligently forward data only to the intended recipient, improving network efficiency and reducing collisions compared to hubs.

Answers

188. **Answer:** A

Explanation: A switch is often referred to as a "multiport repeater" because it operates like a repeater but with multiple ports. Unlike hubs, which repeat incoming signals to all connected devices, switches forward data only to the specific device intended to receive it based on the device's MAC address. This reduces unnecessary traffic on the network and enhances overall network performance.

189. **Answer:** C

Explanation: TCP/IP (Transmission Control Protocol/Internet Protocol) is the foundational protocol suite used in modern networks, including the Internet. It provides end-to-end data communication specifying how data should be packetized, addressed, transmitted, routed, and received between devices on networks. TCP/IP includes protocols like TCP, UDP, IP, and others essential for network communication and internet connectivity.

190. **Answer:** C

Explanation: Firewalls are security devices or software applications that monitor and control incoming and outgoing network traffic based on predetermined security rules or policies. They act as barriers between secured internal networks and untrusted external networks (like the internet), preventing unauthorized access and protecting against threats such as hackers, malware, and unauthorized data transfers. Firewalls can filter traffic based on port numbers, IP addresses, protocols, and application types to enforce security policies and ensure network security.

191. **Answer:** A

Explanation: LAN (Local Area Network) typically covers a small physical area, like a single building or campus, connecting computers and devices within close proximity. WAN (Wide Area Network), on the other hand, covers a large geographic area, often spanning cities, countries, or continents, connecting multiple LANs and other networks.

Copyright © 2024 VERSAtile Reads. All rights reserved.
This material is protected by copyright, any infringement will be dealt with legal and punitive action.

Answers

192. Answer: D

Explanation: A Wireless Access Point (WAP) enables wireless-capable devices (like laptops, smartphones, and tablets) to connect to a wired network using Wi-Fi. It acts as a bridge between wireless devices and the wired LAN, facilitating communication and access to network resources wirelessly.

193. Answer: B

Explanation: DHCP (Dynamic Host Configuration Protocol) automatically assigns IP addresses to devices on a network when they connect, ensuring each device has a unique IP address without manual configuration. It manages IP address allocation, subnet mask, default gateway, DNS server, and other network configuration parameters.

194. Answer: A

Explanation: VLAN (Virtual Local Area Network) is a logically segmented network within a larger physical network. It allows administrators to create multiple virtual networks on a single physical LAN, logically separating traffic and improving network efficiency, security, and management.

195. Answer: A

Explanation: A router is used to segment or divide a network into smaller subnetworks, known as subnets. By routing traffic between different subnets based on IP addresses, routers enable efficient data transmission and improve network performance and security.

196. Answer: B

Explanation: An endpoint refers to any device that communicates directly over a network, such as computers, smartphones, printers, or servers. It is a

Answers

source or destination of data transmitted over the network, interacting with other endpoints to exchange information or access network services.

197. **Answer:** B

Explanation: NAT (Network Address Translation) is used in home routers to convert private IP addresses of devices on a local network into a single public IP address assigned by the ISP (Internet Service Provider). This allows multiple devices to share a single public IP address for internet access, enhancing security and conserving public IP addresses.

198. **Answer:** B

Explanation: A bit (short for binary digit) is the smallest unit of data in computing and networking. It represents a binary value of either 0 or 1, used for digital communication, data storage, and processing in computer networks.

199. **Answer:** C

Explanation: Protocols define rules and standards for how data is formatted, transmitted, received, and acknowledged across a network. They ensure interoperability between different devices and systems by defining a common language and set of procedures for network communication.

200. **Answer:** B

Explanation: SSL (Secure Sockets Layer) and its successor TLS (Transport Layer Security) are cryptographic protocols used to secure communication over a computer network. They encrypt data transmitted between clients and servers, ensuring confidentiality, integrity, and authenticity of the data being exchanged.

201. **Answer:** B

Copyright © 2024 VERSAtile Reads. All rights reserved.
This material is protected by copyright, any infringement will be dealt with legal and punitive action.

Answers

Explanation: Encryption is the process of converting plaintext data into ciphertext to prevent unauthorized access during transmission over a network. It ensures data confidentiality and privacy, protecting sensitive information from interception or eavesdropping.

202. **Answer:** B

Explanation: SSL (Secure Sockets Layer) and TLS (Transport Layer Security) are cryptographic protocols that provide secure communication over a computer network. They establish an encrypted link between a web server and a browser, ensuring data security and integrity during transmission.

203. **Answer:** B

Explanation: SSL/TLS (Secure Sockets Layer/Transport Layer Security) is used to secure HTTP (Hypertext Transfer Protocol) connections, creating a secure channel for data exchange between clients and servers on the internet.

204. **Answer:** B

Explanation: Encryption transforms readable plaintext data into unreadable ciphertext using cryptographic algorithms. This process ensures that only authorized parties with the decryption key can access and interpret the original data.

205. **Answer:** C

Explanation: HTTP (Hypertext Transfer Protocol) is a protocol used for transmitting hypertext requests and responses over the Internet. It operates over TCP (Transmission Control Protocol) port 80 by default. HTTP is considered nonsecure because it does not encrypt the data transmitted between the client (such as a web browser) and the server, making it susceptible to interception and manipulation by malicious actors.

Copyright © 2024 VERSAtile Reads. All rights reserved.
This material is protected by copyright, any infringement will be dealt with legal and punitive action.

Answers

206. **Answer:** C

Explanation: SSL (Secure Sockets Layer) and its successor TLS (Transport Layer Security) are cryptographic protocols designed to provide secure communication over a computer network. They encrypt data transmitted between a client and a server, preventing attackers from eavesdropping on or tampering with the communication. Man-in-the-middle attacks involve intercepting and altering messages between two parties, which SSL/TLS helps prevent by ensuring the integrity and confidentiality of data.

207. **Answer:** C

Explanation: When transmitting data across a network, security is a critical concern. Data transmitted over networks can be intercepted, manipulated, or stolen by unauthorized entities without appropriate security measures in place. Ensuring data confidentiality, integrity, and availability are fundamental aspects of network security.

208. **Answer:** C

Explanation: SSH (Secure Shell) is a protocol used for secure remote login and command execution over an insecure network. It provides strong encryption and authentication mechanisms, making it suitable for secure administration and file transfer activities. Unlike Telnet, which transmits data in plaintext, SSH encrypts all communication between the client and server, thereby protecting it from eavesdropping and unauthorized access.

209. **Answer:** C

Explanation: HTTPS is an extension of HTTP (Hypertext Transfer Protocol) used for secure communication over a computer network. It uses SSL/TLS protocols to encrypt data transmitted between a web browser and a server, ensuring the confidentiality and integrity of the information exchanged. The

Answers

"Secure" in HTTPS denotes the added security features compared to standard HTTP.

210. **Answer:** B

Explanation: A logical port is a software-based entity that represents a specific endpoint of communication in a network. It is identified by a numerical value (port number) that is associated with a particular protocol (e.g., TCP or UDP). Logical ports allow multiple services or applications to operate concurrently on a single network device by directing incoming data to the appropriate application or service based on the port number.

211. **Answer:** C

Explanation: Logging and monitoring are critical for recording and auditing actions performed on data. They provide visibility into system activities and help detect and investigate security incidents by maintaining detailed records of user and system actions.

212. **Answer:** B

Explanation: Both ports in networking and phone extensions in telephony serve as identifiers that direct communications to specific services or individuals within a larger network or system. In networking, a port number directs data packets to the appropriate application or service running on a device. Similarly, a phone extension directs incoming calls to a specific phone line or individual within an organization. Both mechanisms enhance communication efficiency and organization within their respective domains.

213. **Answer:** C

Explanation: In networking, a socket refers to the combination of an IP address and a port number. Together, they uniquely identify a communication endpoint between two devices in a network. A socket allows applications on different devices to establish connections and exchange data

Answers

by specifying both the destination IP address and the specific port number associated with the desired service or application.

214. **Answer:** D

Explanation: The Zero Trust model operates on the principle of "Always Verify, Never Trust," which means that no user or device is automatically trusted, whether inside or outside the network. Every request must be verified before granting access to resources, regardless of its origin.

215. **Answer:** B

Explanation: Servers often host multiple services or applications that require simultaneous communication with clients. Different port numbers are assigned to each service on a server to differentiate between these services. When a client initiates a communication request, it specifies both the server's IP address and the port number associated with the desired service. This allows a single server to manage multiple types of communication requests concurrently without confusion or conflict.

216. **Answer:** C

Explanation: When a client initiates a communication session with a server, it specifies the desired service or application by including the server's port number in the communication request. The port number, along with the server's IP address, identifies the specific endpoint or service to which the client wishes to connect. This enables the client to establish a targeted connection and interact with the intended service on the server.

217. **Answer:** C

Explanation: To distinguish between multiple services running on the same computer (such as a web server and a file transfer server), each service must be assigned a unique port number. For example, HTTP typically uses port 80 for web traffic, while FTP (File Transfer Protocol) uses port 21 for file

Answers

transfers. By assigning different port numbers to each service, the computer can manage incoming connections and direct them to the appropriate service or application based on the

218. **Answer:** D

Explanation: Risk transfer involves shifting the responsibility for managing risk to another party, such as through insurance or outsourcing. This strategy helps mitigate potential financial losses or operational impacts by leveraging external resources or agreements.

219. **Answer:** C

Explanation: A Security Operations Center (SOC) is responsible for continuous monitoring, detecting, and responding to security threats and incidents in real-time. It acts as the central hub for managing security events and coordinating responses to maintain the organization's security posture.

220. **Answer:** C

Explanation: The attack surface encompasses all the points in a system that an attacker could target. This includes network interfaces, applications, and services. Reducing the attack surface involves minimizing these potential entry points to decrease vulnerability.

221. **Answer:** C

Explanation: The General Data Protection Regulation (GDPR) is a regulation in the European Union designed to protect personal data and privacy. It mandates strict guidelines for data collection, storage, and processing to ensure individuals' privacy rights are upheld.

222. **Answer:** B

Answers

Explanation: Network segmentation involves dividing a network into smaller segments or zones to contain security breaches and limit their impact. It helps reduce the attack surface and prevent attackers from moving laterally across the network if a breach occurs.

223. **Answer:** B

Explanation: Hashing generates a unique fixed-size hash value for data, which can be used to verify its integrity. If the hash value changes, it indicates that the data has been altered. Hashing ensures that the data remains unchanged during storage or transmission.

224. **Answer:** B

Explanation: STRIDE is a threat modeling methodology that helps identify potential threats by focusing on the attacker's perspective. It categorizes threats into Spoofing, Tampering, Repudiation, Information Disclosure, Denial of Service, and Elevation of Privilege, helping to evaluate security from various angles.

225. **Answer:** A

Explanation: Cross-Site Scripting (XSS) attacks exploit the trust a user's browser has in a website by injecting malicious scripts into web pages viewed by other users. This can lead to the theft of session cookies, sensitive data, or other harmful effects.

226. **Answer:** A

Explanation: The NIST Cybersecurity Framework (CSF) offers a comprehensive approach to managing and improving cybersecurity practices. It is designed to help organizations align their cybersecurity activities with business needs and regulatory requirements, providing a structured approach to security control management.

Copyright © 2024 VERSAtile Reads. All rights reserved.
This material is protected by copyright, any infringement will be dealt with legal and punitive action.

Answers

227. **Answer:** C

Explanation: The Network Layer (Layer 3) of the OSI model is responsible for routing and route selection for network packets. It manages logical addressing, determines the best path for data packets to reach their destination across interconnected networks, and ensures efficient and reliable communication. Routing protocols such as RIP, OSPF, and BGP operate at this layer to facilitate dynamic routing decisions based on network topology and conditions.

228. **Answer:** C

Explanation: Routers are the primary devices associated with the Network Layer (Layer 3) of the OSI model. They are responsible for forwarding data packets between different networks based on IP addresses and making intelligent routing decisions to ensure data reaches its destination efficiently. Routers enable interconnectivity and communication across diverse network environments, playing a critical role in directing traffic and optimizing network performance.

229. **Answer:** C

Explanation: A Layer 3 switch combines the functionality of a traditional Layer 2 switch (Data Link Layer) with routing capabilities similar to those of a router (Network Layer). Layer 3 switches can perform routing tasks based on IP addresses, allowing them to forward data packets between different networks or VLANs (Virtual LANs) within a local area network (LAN). These switches optimize traffic flow and improve network efficiency by handling routing and switching functions in a single device.

230. **Answer:** C

Explanation: TCP (Transmission Control Protocol) operates at the Transport Layer (Layer 4) of the OSI model, not the Network Layer (Layer

Answers

3). TCP is responsible for reliable, connection-oriented communication between applications, ensuring data integrity and flow control. In contrast, the Network Layer focuses on routing packets between source and destination devices using logical addressing (such as IP addresses) and managing data delivery across networks.

231. **Answer:** B

Explanation: The Network Layer primarily uses logical IP addresses for routing. IP addresses are hierarchical and provide a scalable addressing scheme, allowing routers to direct packets across networks.

232. **Answer:** C

Explanation: The primary function of the Network Layer in the OSI model is routing and route selection. It determines the best path for data packets through interconnected networks based on network conditions and routing protocols.

233. **Answer:** C

Explanation: Hubs do not operate at the Network Layer; they operate at the Physical Layer. Hubs repeat signals and do not perform any routing or network layer functions.

234. **Answer:** B

Explanation: ICMP (Internet Control Message Protocol) is used for error reporting and diagnostics at the Network Layer. It handles messages such as "Destination Unreachable" or "Time Exceeded" to troubleshoot network issues.

235. **Answer:** B

Answers

Explanation: Routing protocols at the Network Layer are designed to select the most efficient paths for data transmission between networks based on factors like network topology and traffic load.

236. **Answer:** A

Explanation: Command Injection vulnerabilities occur when user input is improperly handled, allowing attackers to execute arbitrary commands on a system. This can lead to unauthorized access, data manipulation, or system compromise.

237. **Answer:** B

Explanation: The primary responsibility of the Data Link Layer is to manage the transmission and delivery of data frames within a Local Area Network (LAN), using MAC addresses for addressing and error detection.

238. **Answer:** B

Explanation: The Data Link Layer is composed of two sublayers: Logical Link Control (LLC) and Media Access Control (MAC). LLC manages communication links, and MAC handles physical addressing and access to the network medium.

239. **Answer:** C

Explanation: ARP (Address Resolution Protocol) operates at the Data Link Layer. It resolves IP addresses to MAC addresses within a local network segment, facilitating communication between devices.

240. **Answer:** C

Explanation: LLC stands for Logical Link Control in the context of the Data Link Layer. It manages error checking, flow control, and synchronization of

Answers

data frames within a LAN, ensuring reliable communication between devices.

241. **Answer:** C

Explanation: IEEE 802.11 corresponds to wireless Ethernet standards, commonly known as Wi-Fi. It defines protocols for wireless local area networks (WLANs) and enables wireless connectivity between devices.

242. **Answer:** C

Explanation: During the Containment phase of incident response, the goal is to prevent the incident from spreading and causing further damage. This involves isolating affected systems, halting malicious activities, and controlling the situation to protect unaffected parts of the network.

243. **Answer:** C

Explanation: Fault Tolerance refers to designing systems with redundancy to ensure they continue operating even if one or more components fail. This concept is crucial for maintaining service availability and reliability in critical systems.

244. **Answer:** B

Explanation: The MAC (Media Access Control) sublayer in the Data Link Layer is responsible for defining and managing physical MAC addresses. It handles how devices on a network access and share the physical medium.

245. **Answer:** B

Explanation: IP (Internet Protocol) operates at the Network Layer (Layer 3) of the OSI model, not at the Data Link Layer. Data Link Layer standards include Ethernet (IEEE 802.3) and Wireless Ethernet (IEEE 802.11).

Copyright © 2024 VERSAtile Reads. All rights reserved.
This material is protected by copyright, any infringement will be dealt with legal and punitive action.

Answers

246. **Answer:** C

Explanation: The Diffie-Hellman algorithm is used for securely exchanging symmetric encryption keys over an insecure channel. It enables two parties to establish a shared secret key that can be used for subsequent encrypted communications.

247. **Answer:** C

Explanation: SSH (Secure Shell) is commonly used for securely logging into Unix/Linux computers over a network. It provides encrypted communication and secure authentication methods.

248. **Answer:** B

Explanation: SSH provides a text-based Command-Line Interface (CLI) for interacting with Unix/Linux computers remotely. It allows users to execute commands and manage the system securely.

249. **Answer:** B

Explanation: SSH typically runs over port 22. This port number is standardized for SSH communication, ensuring consistency and ease of configuration.

250. **Answer:** C

Explanation: Telnet is known for its lack of security compared to SSH. It transmits data over the network in plaintext, making it vulnerable to interception and unauthorized access.

251. **Answer:** B

Answers

Explanation: IoT stands for Internet of Things, referring to a network of interconnected devices embedded with sensors, software, and connectivity to exchange data and perform tasks autonomously.

252. **Answer:** B

Explanation: IoT devices are called smart devices because they have processing capabilities, sensors, and automated functionalities that enable them to perform tasks intelligently and autonomously.

253. **Answer:** D

Explanation: Traditional desktop computing is not a common application of IoT devices. IoT applications are more focused on automation, industrial control, consumer electronics, and smart home devices.

254. **Answer:** B

Explanation: Weak authentication mechanisms, such as default passwords or lack of two-factor authentication, are common security vulnerabilities in IoT devices. Attackers can exploit them to gain unauthorized access.

255. **Answer:** B

Explanation: Changing default settings, such as passwords and configurations, is a compensating control for IoT devices. It reduces the risk of exploitation by ensuring that devices are not using vulnerable default configurations.

256. **Answer:** B

Explanation: Physical access is a security issue for IoT devices because many of them are deployed in diverse and uncontrolled environments where securing physical access can be difficult or impractical.

Copyright © 2024 VERSAtile Reads. All rights reserved.
This material is protected by copyright, any infringement will be dealt with legal and punitive action.

Answers

257. **Answer:** B

Explanation: The primary purpose of a security program assessment is to assess and evaluate how effective an organization's security measures, policies, and controls are in protecting its assets and mitigating risks.

258. **Answer:** B

Explanation: Security assessments and testing are often conducted by independent auditors or third-party firms with expertise in cybersecurity. They provide impartial evaluations and recommendations to improve an organization's security posture.

259. **Answer:** D

Explanation: Installing new hardware is not typically part of a security program assessment. Assessments focus more on evaluating existing security controls, policies, compliance with regulations, and identifying vulnerabilities.

260. **Answer:** A

Explanation: Encryption at Rest involves encrypting data stored in cloud infrastructure to protect it from unauthorized access. This technique ensures that even if data is compromised, it remains unreadable without the appropriate decryption key, addressing confidentiality concerns in a shared environment.

261. **Answer:** B

Explanation: On-premises refers to data centers that are owned, managed, and operated by the organization itself, located within its physical premises. Cloud data centers, on the other hand, are operated and managed by Cloud Service Providers (CSPs) and accessed via the internet.

Copyright © 2024 VERSAtile Reads. All rights reserved.
This material is protected by copyright, any infringement will be dealt with legal and punitive action.

Answers

262. Answer: C

Explanation: One of the key differences between on-premises and cloud infrastructure is how services are provisioned, managed, and utilized. On-premises infrastructure requires organizations to purchase and maintain hardware and software themselves, while cloud infrastructure provides scalable and on-demand access to resources managed by a third-party provider.

263. Answer: D

Explanation: Managing an on-premises data center typically involves roles such as facilities manager, safety officer, and IT personnel who handle the physical infrastructure, security, and IT operations of the data center.

264. Answer: B

Explanation: HVAC systems in data centers are crucial for maintaining optimal environmental conditions, including temperature and humidity, to ensure the efficient operation and longevity of IT equipment.

265. Answer: B

Explanation: Network redundancy in a data center involves having multiple network communication paths and components to ensure uninterrupted connectivity. It helps prevent downtime and ensures reliable access to applications and services.

266. Answer: C

Explanation: Power redundancy in data centers is typically achieved using backup systems such as batteries (uninterruptible power supply or UPS) and electric generators. These systems provide backup power in case of primary power source failures.

Answers

267. **Answer:** C

Explanation: A security program assessment typically includes components such as a security policy review, data security review, and incident handling review, focusing on evaluating and improving an organization's overall security posture.

268. **Answer:** B

Explanation: Penetration testing (pen testing) aims to identify vulnerabilities in an organization's IT infrastructure and simulate cyberattacks to demonstrate how these vulnerabilities can be exploited. It helps organizations understand their security weaknesses and prioritize remediation efforts.

269. **Answer:** D

Explanation: Vulnerability assessments typically include network and system vulnerability testing, application security assessment, and physical security assessment. "Marketing vulnerability assessment" is not a recognized type of vulnerability assessment.

270. **Answer:** C

Explanation: Security policies regarding IoT devices should address their proper usage, secure configuration practices, and regular security testing to mitigate potential risks associated with these interconnected devices.

271. **Answer:** C

Explanation: Redundancy of supply systems, including power and network redundancies, is critical for ensuring continuous operations in data centers. It minimizes the risk of downtime due to equipment failures or power outages.

Answers

272. **Answer:** B

Explanation: Service Level Agreements (SLAs) define the terms of service provision, including uptime guarantees, response times for issue resolution, and procedures for service restoration in case of outages.

273. **Answer:** B

Explanation: Business Impact Analysis (BIA) is a process used to identify and prioritize critical business functions and their dependencies, including the level of redundancy required to ensure continuity in case of disruptions.

274. **Answer:** C

Explanation: Hardware redundancy in a data center involves having duplicate or backup hardware components such as servers, storage devices, and networking equipment to ensure continued operation in case of hardware failures.

275. **Answer:** C

Explanation: Power outages in data centers can be caused by severe weather conditions, equipment failures (such as UPS or generator failures), and physical damage to power systems. Software malfunctions typically do not directly cause power outages.

276. **Answer:** B

Explanation: A UPS in a data center provides temporary power during short-term power outages or until backup power systems (such as generators) can be activated. It helps prevent interruptions to critical IT operations.

Answers

277. **Answer:** B

Explanation: Reciprocal agreements between organizations allow them to provide mutual aid and resources during emergencies or disasters, enhancing their collective ability to respond and recover.

278. **Answer:** C

Explanation: Preventative maintenance in data center operations involves regular inspections, testing, and maintenance of equipment and systems to identify and address potential issues proactively. It helps optimize performance and reduce the risk of unplanned downtime.

279. **Answer:** C

Explanation: The National Institute of Standards and Technology (NIST) defines cloud computing as a model for enabling ubiquitous, convenient, on-demand network access to a shared pool of configurable computing resources (e.g., networks, servers, storage, applications, and services) that can be rapidly provisioned and released with minimal management effort or service provider interaction.

280. **Answer:** C

Explanation: On-demand self-service is a characteristic of cloud computing that allows customers to provision and manage computing resources, such as server instances and storage, without requiring human intervention from the service provider. Users can dynamically adjust their resource usage based on demand.

281. **Answer:** B

Explanation: In the PaaS (Platform as a Service) cloud service model, the cloud provider manages the infrastructure and middleware, while the customer manages applications, data, and application settings. This model

Answers

provides greater flexibility and control over applications and platforms compared to SaaS (Software as a Service).

282. **Answer:** B

Explanation: Multitenancy in cloud computing refers to the practice of allocating and sharing physical and virtualized cloud resources (such as servers and storage) among multiple tenants (customers or users). Each tenant's data and applications are logically isolated and segregated to ensure privacy, security, and compliance.

283. **Answer:** D

Explanation: A private cloud deployment model is exclusive to a single organization, either hosted internally or externally by a dedicated provider. It offers greater control, security, and customization compared to public or hybrid clouds, catering specifically to the organization's needs and requirements.

284. **Answer:** A

Explanation: Security posture refers to the overall effectiveness of an organization's security measures, including policies, controls, and practices. It reflects the organization's ability to protect against and respond to security threats.

285. **Answer:** B

Explanation: A Service Level Agreement (SLA) is a contractual agreement between a service provider and a customer that defines the level of service, performance metrics, responsibilities, and guarantees regarding the service provided. It ensures clarity and accountability in service delivery.

286. **Answer:** B

Answers

Explanation: SOC 2 (Service Organization Control 2) focuses on security, availability, processing integrity, confidentiality, and privacy controls. It provides a framework for evaluating and reporting on controls relevant to the security, availability, and confidentiality of data processed by Cloud Service Providers (CSPs).

287. **Answer:** C

Explanation: A hybrid cloud combines public and private clouds, allowing data and applications to be shared between them. It offers flexibility and scalability by leveraging both on-premises and off-premises resources.

288. **Answer:** B

Explanation: Organizations using Cloud Service Providers (CSPs) are primarily concerned with ensuring that the CSP implements robust security practices to protect their data and applications from unauthorized access, breaches, and other security threats.

289. **Answer:** A

Explanation: SOC 1 (Service Organization Control 1) audits focus on controls relevant to financial reporting, typically for organizations that provide services that could impact their clients' financial statements.

290. **Answer:** B

Explanation: Rapid elasticity in cloud computing refers to the ability to quickly scale resources up or down based on demand. This characteristic allows organizations to efficiently manage varying workloads and optimize resource utilization.

291. **Answer:** B

Answers

Explanation: The CSA STAR (Security, Trust, Assurance, and Risk) program helps CSPs document their security practices through the STAR registry, providing transparency and enabling customers to assess the security posture of different CSPs.

292. **Answer:** C

Explanation: The CSA STAR Registry provides a list of CSPs and their associated security assurance levels based on self-assessment against CSA's Cloud Controls Matrix (CCM) and other criteria.

293. **Answer:** B

Explanation: Data creation is the initial phase where data is generated or acquired by an organization. It marks the beginning of the data lifecycle, which includes stages like storage, processing, analysis, and eventual deletion or archival.

294. **Answer:** C

Explanation: Organizations can acquire data from external sources (other organizations, vendors, etc.) or generate it internally through their operations, processes, and interactions.

295. **Answer:** B

Explanation: Once data exists within an organization, a key consideration is ensuring it is protected appropriately to prevent unauthorized access, breaches, and data loss.

296. **Answer:** B

Explanation: Encryption is a method of data protection that converts data into a form that can only be read or processed with the correct decryption

Answers

key. It ensures data confidentiality and security during storage, transit, and processing.

297. **Answer:** C

Explanation: Data sharing involves distributing data among authorized users or systems, not protecting it. Methods like access controls, encryption, and monitoring are used to protect data.

298. **Answer:** A

Explanation: Organizations must consider privacy concerns related to how data may be used, accessed, shared, and stored to comply with legal regulations and ethical standards.

299. **Answer:** B

Explanation: Monitoring data access ensures that only authorized individuals or systems can access and manipulate data, enhancing data security and preventing unauthorized activities.

300. **Answer:** B

Explanation: Access controls are necessary to regulate and manage who can access data, ensuring that only authorized users or systems can view, modify, or delete sensitive information.

301. **Answer:** A

Explanation: Data destruction involves securely deleting data that is no longer needed. Before destruction, organizations must decide on appropriate methods to protect data privacy and prevent unauthorized recovery.

Answers

302. **Answer:** B

Explanation: Considering privacy requirements ensures that organizations handle data in accordance with legal regulations and ethical standards, protecting individuals' rights and preventing data breaches.

303. **Answer:** B

Explanation: Data classification categorizes data based on sensitivity, importance, and other criteria to apply appropriate security controls and ensure data protection, confidentiality, and compliance.

304. **Answer:** C

Explanation: The risk associated with data determines its classification level, considering factors such as sensitivity, regulatory requirements, and potential impact if compromised.

305. **Answer:** C

Explanation: Top Secret is an example of a high sensitivity classification level indicating highly confidential information requiring the strictest security controls and limited access.

306. **Answer:** B

Explanation: The classification level of data dictates the appropriate security controls needed to protect it, ensuring that measures align with the sensitivity and importance of the information.

307. **Answer:** C

Explanation: Classified data is typically marked with labels, tags, or metadata indicating its classification level and the required security controls, ensuring proper handling and protection.

Copyright © 2024 VERSAtile Reads. All rights reserved.
This material is protected by copyright, any infringement will be dealt with legal and punitive action.

Answers

308. **Answer:** D

Explanation: Physical media such as storage devices or documents can be labeled using stickers or other marking methods to indicate their classification level and ensure appropriate handling and protection.

309. **Answer:** C

Explanation: Unrestricted data classification typically requires stringent access controls to prevent unauthorized access and ensure data security despite being less sensitive compared to classified or proprietary data.

310. **Answer:** B

Explanation: Data classification helps ensure that sensitive data receives the necessary protection and is accessed only by authorized personnel, reducing the risk of unauthorized disclosure or misuse.

311. **Answer:** B

Explanation: Deleting data is not typically an action taken after classifying data. Instead, data deletion occurs when data is no longer needed or has reached the end of its lifecycle. Classification helps in determining the appropriate level of protection and management for data throughout its lifecycle, including encryption, access controls, and monitoring.

312. **Answer:** B

Explanation: Not properly labeling classified data can lead to unauthorized access. Proper labeling ensures that data is recognized and handled according to its sensitivity level, preventing unauthorized individuals from accessing it. This is crucial for maintaining data security and compliance with organizational policies and regulations.

Answers

313. **Answer:** B

Explanation: Data security aims to protect information important to the organization, including sensitive business data, customer information, intellectual property, and operational details. It ensures that this information is safeguarded against unauthorized access, breaches, and threats, maintaining confidentiality, integrity, and availability.

314. **Answer:** B

Explanation: Public news articles generally do not contain sensitive or confidential information that requires protection. In contrast, employee records, sensitive customer data, and confidential company information are examples of information that organizations typically need to protect from unauthorized access and disclosure.

315. **Answer:** A

Explanation: Data security measures aim to protect information from unauthorized access, modification, and disclosure. This includes preventing unauthorized users from accessing sensitive data, ensuring data integrity against alterations, and safeguarding confidentiality by controlling who can view or use the data.

316. **Answer:** B

Explanation: Technical measures in data security controls involve the use of computer hardware (such as firewalls and intrusion detection systems) and software (like encryption and antivirus programs) to protect data from unauthorized access and breaches. These measures are essential for ensuring the security and integrity of data stored and transmitted within an organization.

317. **Answer:** A

Answers

Explanation: (ISC)2 CC candidates who are preparing for cybersecurity certifications need to be aware of key data security practices. These practices include implementing technical measures, enforcing access controls, and monitoring data usage to protect sensitive information.

318. **Answer:** B

Explanation: Employee records are considered confidential information that requires protection. This includes personal details, payroll information, and performance evaluations, which need to be safeguarded against unauthorized access and disclosure to ensure privacy and compliance with data protection laws.

319. **Answer:** A

Explanation: Data security controls primarily involve technical measures such as encryption, firewalls, access controls, and intrusion detection systems. These measures are implemented to protect data from unauthorized access, ensure data integrity, and maintain confidentiality.

320. **Answer:** B

Explanation: The primary focus of data security practices is to protect information from unauthorized access, modification, and disclosure. This includes implementing security controls, educating employees on security best practices, and adhering to compliance requirements to safeguard sensitive data.

321. **Answer:** B

Explanation: "Confidential company information" typically refers to intellectual property, which includes trade secrets, patents, and proprietary business processes. Protecting intellectual property is crucial for maintaining a competitive advantage and preventing unauthorized use or disclosure.

Answers

322. **Answer:** A

Explanation: To protect sensitive information, organizations must implement data security controls such as encryption, access controls, and data masking. These controls help mitigate risks associated with data breaches and ensure compliance with data protection regulations.

323. **Answer:** B

Explanation: The purpose of archiving data is to retain it for future reference, legal requirements, or historical preservation. Archived data is stored securely and can be retrieved if needed for audits, investigations, or compliance purposes.

324. **Answer:** D

Explanation: A flash drive is not typically mentioned as a type of data archival media. Common types of data archival media include tape, disk, and optical media, which are used for long-term storage and backup purposes.

325. **Answer:** B

Explanation: Data retention involves storing data that is no longer needed for current business operations but must be retained for compliance, legal, or historical reasons. This ensures that organizations can access and retrieve data if required in the future.

326. **Answer:** B

Explanation: Organizations may need to retain data even if it is no longer needed for operational purposes to comply with legal and regulatory requirements. These requirements dictate how long certain types of data must be retained before it can be securely deleted or archived.

Copyright © 2024 VERSAtile Reads. All rights reserved.
This material is protected by copyright, any infringement will be dealt with legal and punitive action.

Answers

327. **Answer:** C

Explanation: Data archival can be implemented using both on-premises and cloud solutions. On-premises solutions involve storing archived data locally, while cloud solutions offer scalable storage options and remote accessibility for archived data.

328. **Answer:** C

Explanation: Data retention laws mandate organizations to retain data for specified periods to meet legal, regulatory, or industry requirements. These laws vary by jurisdiction and apply to both digital and physical data formats.

329. **Answer:** B

Explanation: When data is no longer needed for current operations but must be retained, it is typically archived rather than permanently deleted. Archiving ensures that data remains accessible for compliance, historical, or reference purposes.

330. **Answer:** B

Explanation: Vulnerability Assessment involves regularly scanning systems for vulnerabilities and applying fixes or mitigations as part of an ongoing process. It helps organizations identify and address weaknesses before they can be exploited by attackers, supporting continuous improvement in security.

331. **Answer:** B

Explanation: One of the primary purposes of data archival is to meet legal and regulatory requirements for retaining data over specific periods. This ensures that organizations comply with laws governing data protection, privacy, and auditing.

Answers

332. **Answer:** A

Explanation: Data archival can be performed using cloud implementations. Cloud storage provides scalable, cost-effective solutions for long-term data retention, offering accessibility, redundancy, and compliance with archival needs.

333. **Answer:** A

Explanation: When data is deleted by pressing the DELETE key on a computer, it is typically permanently removed from the hard drive. However, recovery may still be possible with specialized tools until the space is overwritten.

334. **Answer:** A

Explanation: Emptying the recycle bin on your desktop permanently erases the data from the hard drive by freeing up the space previously occupied by the deleted files. This action makes the data unrecoverable through normal means.

335. **Answer:** A

Explanation: Free data recovery tools can easily recover data that has been deleted or emptied from the recycle bin, as long as the new data has not overwritten the space. These tools scan the disk for traces of deleted files and restore them.

336. **Answer:** B

Explanation: Sanitization is the term used to describe the process of ensuring that sensitive data cannot be recovered from media. This process may involve overwriting data multiple times, degaussing magnetic media, or physically destroying storage devices.

Answers

337. **Answer:** B

Explanation: Overwriting is a method of sanitization where new data is written over existing data multiple times to make it unrecoverable. This process ensures that the data recovery tools or techniques cannot retrieve the original data.

338. **Answer:** B

Explanation: In the context of data sanitization, overwriting involves writing new data over the old data multiple times to prevent recovery. This method is effective in ensuring that sensitive information cannot be retrieved from storage media.

339. **Answer:** B

Explanation: Degaussing is a sanitization method that uses magnetic fields to erase data from magnetic storage media, such as hard drives and magnetic tapes. It disrupts the magnetic domains on the media, rendering the data unrecoverable.

340. **Answer:** B

Explanation: The primary requirement when data is no longer needed is to ensure that sensitive data cannot be recovered. This involves securely deleting or sanitizing the data using methods like overwriting, degaussing, or physical destruction.

341. **Answer:** A

Explanation: Physical destruction of media involves physically shredding or breaking storage devices into pieces to ensure that data stored on them cannot be accessed or recovered. This method is effective for ensuring data security when media is no longer needed.

Answers

342. **Answer:** D

Explanation: Moving data to the recycle bin is not a method of sanitization. Data in the recycle bin can be easily recovered until it is permanently deleted or emptied from the recycle bin.

343. **Answer:** C

Explanation: The Firewall Rule Set consists of the rules and policies configured on a firewall to control which network traffic is permitted or blocked. It is crucial for defining and enforcing the security boundaries of a network.

344. **Answer:** C

Explanation: Zeroization is another term used for data overwriting in the context of data sanitization. It refers to the process of replacing existing data with zeros or other patterns to prevent recovery of the original data.

345. **Answer:** D

Explanation: Using color codes is not a method used for overwriting data. Overwriting typically involves replacing existing data with new data patterns, such as zeros, ones, or random data, to prevent recovery.

346. **Answer:** B

Explanation: Increasing the number of passes in data overwriting makes the original data harder to recover. Multiple passes overwrite the data multiple times with new patterns, reducing the likelihood of recovery by data recovery tools.

347. **Answer:** B

Answers

Explanation: In the context of data overwriting, a "pass" refers to a single instance of data being overwritten with new data patterns. Multiple passes involve repeating this process several times to ensure data security.

348. **Answer:** C

Explanation: Random data is used in the process of overwriting to ensure that the original data is harder to recover. Overwriting with random patterns makes it more difficult for data recovery tools to reconstruct the original information.

349. **Answer:** B

Explanation: Multiple passes are generally more secure for data overwriting compared to a single pass. Multiple passes increase the complexity of data recovery, as each pass overwrites the data with new patterns, making it harder to reconstruct the original information.

350. **Answer:** C

Explanation: Data clearing is another term used for zeroization in the context of data overwriting. It refers to the process of clearing or erasing data from storage media to ensure that it cannot be recovered.

351. **Answer:** B

Explanation: Overwriting data only once may still leave traces of the original data recoverable through advanced data recovery techniques. Multiple passes of overwriting are typically needed to make the original data much harder or practically impossible to recover.

352. **Answer:** A

Explanation: Data overwriting is primarily concerned with data security. It involves securely erasing data to prevent unauthorized access or recovery,

Answers

ensuring that sensitive information cannot be retrieved from storage devices.

353. **Answer:** B

Explanation: Encryption is the process of transforming plaintext into ciphertext to secure data during transmission or storage. It ensures that only authorized parties can access and decipher the information.

354. **Answer:** B

Explanation: The primary focus of incident response in cybersecurity is preparing for and responding to security incidents effectively and efficiently. This includes identifying, analyzing, and mitigating cybersecurity threats and attacks.

355. **Answer:** B

Explanation: Business continuity planning primarily aims to ensure that critical business functions can continue to operate during and after a disaster or disruptive event. It focuses on maintaining operations to minimize downtime and financial losses.

356. **Answer:** B

Explanation: The main goal of disaster recovery within an organization is to recover IT systems and information processing capabilities after a disaster or disruptive event. It involves restoring data, applications, and infrastructure to resume normal business operations.

357. **Answer:** B

Explanation: The National Institute of Standards and Technology (NIST) supports the approach where disaster recovery plans take over if incident

Answers

response and business continuity plans fail. NIST provides guidelines and standards for disaster recovery planning.

358. **Answer:** B

Explanation: The consequence of the UK hospital system not having a business continuity plan in 2016 was that 3,000 medical procedures had to be canceled due to a cyberattack. This incident highlighted the importance of having robust business continuity plans in healthcare.

359. **Answer:** C

Explanation: Incident response governance includes establishing policies, procedures, and guidelines for incident detection, response, and recovery. An incident response policy outlines the organization's approach to handling security incidents.

360. **Answer:** B

Explanation: In the context of incident response, an 'event' refers to an occurrence of an activity on an information system that could potentially indicate a security incident or anomaly requiring investigation.

361. **Answer:** B

Explanation: In incident response terminology, an 'exploit' refers to an action or tool that takes advantage of a system vulnerability or weakness to compromise security and gain unauthorized access to systems or data.

362. **Answer:** A

Explanation: The primary purpose of an incident response plan is to outline the organization's approach to incident detection, response, mitigation, and recovery. It provides guidelines and procedures for responding to cybersecurity incidents effectively.

Answers

363. **Answer:** C

Explanation: The preparation phase of the incident response process involves planning and resourcing, including establishing incident response policies, procedures, and resources needed to effectively respond to security incidents.

364. **Answer:** B

Explanation: According to NIST, the first step in the incident response process is preparation. This involves establishing incident response capabilities, policies, and procedures before incidents occur.

365. **Answer:** C

Explanation: The incident response manager or lead is typically responsible for coordinating the activities of the incident response team. They oversee the detection, analysis, containment, eradication, and recovery phases of incident response.

366. **Answer:** C

Explanation: Insourcing in the context of incident response team staffing refers to using in-house personnel and resources to handle incident response activities internally rather than outsourcing them to external consultants or services.

367. **Answer:** C

Explanation: In incident response terminology, a threat actor refers to an entity or individual that carries out attacks or exploits vulnerabilities to compromise systems or data security. A hacker is a common type of threat actor.

Answers

368. **Answer:** B

Explanation: The detection and analysis phase of incident response aims to identify and analyze potential security incidents or anomalies within an organization's IT environment. It involves monitoring and analyzing system logs, alerts, and events.

369. **Answer:** D

Explanation: External media, such as USB drives or CDs, are not typically considered common attack vectors in the same way as web applications, phishing, or social engineering.

370. **Answer:** B

Explanation: Social engineering involves manipulating individuals to perform actions or divulge confidential information, often through deception or psychological manipulation. It exploits human behavior rather than technical vulnerabilities.

371. **Answer:** B

Explanation: Logs in the detection and analysis phase of incident response capture and store events from various systems and applications. They provide a record of activities and incidents for later retrieval, analysis, and investigation.

372. **Answer:** B

Explanation: Security Information and Event Management (SIEM) is a tool that aggregates and correlates event logs from various sources into a central repository. It provides real-time analysis of security alerts and helps detect and respond to security incidents.

373. **Answer:** C

Answers

Explanation: Incident documentation and triage involve documenting and tracking incident investigations, including gathering evidence, analyzing impact, and prioritizing responses based on severity and criticality.

374. **Answer:** B

Explanation: Key elements of incident documentation include detailed records of incident investigations, including contact information for relevant parties, timelines of events, actions taken, and outcomes.

375. **Answer:** D

Explanation: An IDS detects and alerts personnel when an attack may be occurring but does not actively block the attack. It monitors network traffic for suspicious activities or patterns that indicate potential security breaches.

376. **Answer:** A

Explanation: Endpoint isolation is a common method to prevent the spread of an incident beyond the network perimeter. It involves isolating compromised endpoints or devices to contain the impact of an incident and prevent further spread.

377. **Answer:** C

Explanation: Eradication in incident response involves removing an attacker's foothold or presence from the environment after containment. It includes identifying and eliminating the root cause of the incident to prevent recurrence.

378. **Answer:** B

Explanation: The Business Continuity Coordinator is primarily responsible for overseeing the business continuity planning process. They ensure that

Answers

plans are developed, maintained, and tested to ensure the organization's resilience to disruptions.

379. **Answer:** B

Explanation: A Business Impact Analysis (BIA) aims to understand business functions, processes, and dependencies to identify critical systems and prioritize their restoration after a disaster. It assesses the potential impact of disruptions on business operations.

380. **Answer:** B

Explanation: Employee salary reviews are not typically a component of a business continuity project plan. A business continuity project plan typically includes project goals, requirements, schedules, milestones, deliverables, and work products related to maintaining business continuity during and after disruptions.

381. **Answer:** A

Explanation: MTD stands for Maximum Tolerable Downtime in the context of business continuity planning. It represents the maximum amount of time an organization can afford to be without its critical business functions or IT services after a disaster or disruption.

382. **Answer:** C

Explanation: Typically, the Marketing Department is not directly involved in a business continuity plan committee. The committee usually comprises representatives from IT, Security, Legal, and other critical departments responsible for business operations and continuity.

383. **Answer:** B

Answers

Explanation: In a phased approach to business continuity planning, the initial phase is usually focused on creating a plan for a portion of the organization. This approach allows for a systematic and manageable implementation of business continuity measures.

384. **Answer:** B

Explanation: Fortification of facilities is an example of preventive control in business continuity planning. It involves physical security measures to protect critical facilities and infrastructure from potential threats or disruptions.

385. **Answer:** C

Explanation: After obtaining management buy-in for a business continuity plan, the next step is typically to form a business continuity plan committee. This committee is responsible for developing, implementing, and maintaining the business continuity plan.

386. **Answer:** B

Explanation: It is important to place business continuity documentation under configuration control to track changes and ensure that the latest procedures and plans are used during a disaster or disruption. This helps maintain consistency and readiness.

387. **Answer:** C

Explanation: Calculating the risk for each business function is not typically part of performing a Business Impact Analysis (BIA). Instead, a BIA focuses on identifying critical business functions, assessing their dependencies, and determining recovery priorities.

388. **Answer:** B

Answers

Explanation: The purpose of the Business Impact Analysis (BIA) in Business Continuity Management (BCM) is to identify the priorities, critical resources, minimum acceptable downtimes, and recovery times for essential business functions.

389. **Answer:** C

Explanation: Recovery strategies in business continuity planning typically address categories such as business process recovery, facility recovery, and data recovery. Customer satisfaction recovery is not typically a category addressed separately in recovery strategies.

390. **Answer:** B

Explanation: RTO stands for Recovery Time Objective in the context of BCM. It defines the maximum acceptable downtime for business processes or IT systems after a disruption before the organization can resume normal operations.

391. **Answer:** C

Explanation: Structured walk-through testing involves reviewing the business continuity plan by a group of representatives from each department. It allows for a comprehensive review and validation of the plan's effectiveness and coordination.

392. **Answer:** A

Explanation: A hot site is fully equipped and configured with up-to-date hardware, software, and data, ready for immediate use in case of a disaster. It provides a quick and seamless transition for critical business operations.

393. **Answer:** B

Answers

Explanation: WRT stands for Work Response Time in the context of BCM. It refers to the time it takes for business operations to resume after a disruption or disaster, ensuring minimal impact on business continuity.

394. **Answer:** B

Explanation: Full-interruption testing involves shutting down the operational site to simulate an actual disaster scenario. It tests the organization's readiness to activate the business continuity plan and recover operations under extreme conditions.

395. **Answer:** A

Explanation: The primary focus of a Disaster Recovery Plan (DRP) is to ensure the continuity and recovery of IT systems, data, and communications functions after a disaster or disruptive event.

396. **Answer:** C

Explanation: A cold site is an empty building or facility that requires significant setup, including installation of equipment, data restoration, and configuration before it can be used as an operational site during a disaster recovery scenario.

397. **Answer:** B

Explanation: It is important to maintain security during the activation of a Disaster Recovery Plan (DRP) to ensure the confidentiality, availability, and integrity of resources and data during recovery operations.

398. **Answer:** B

Explanation: A LAN (Local Area Network) enables network communication between computing devices within limited facilities, such as a building, office, or campus, allowing for data and resource sharing.

Answers

399. **Answer:** C

Explanation: A wireless LAN is commonly referred to as WLAN (Wireless Local Area Network). It provides network communication between computing devices using wireless signals instead of wired connections.

400. **Answer:** C

Explanation: LANs (Local Area Networks) typically cover limited geographic areas, such as a building, office, or campus. They can be configured with both wired (Ethernet) and wireless (Wi-Fi) technologies to connect computing devices within the same physical location.

401. **Answer:** B

Explanation: Digital Signatures are used to verify the authenticity and integrity of data during transmission. They provide a way to ensure that the data has not been altered and that it comes from a legitimate source.

402. **Answer:** B

Explanation: An Advanced Persistent Threat (APT) is a sophisticated and sustained cyberattack carried out by highly skilled adversaries. It focuses on gaining unauthorized access to sensitive information over a prolonged period, often targeting specific organizations or sectors.

403. **Answer:** A

Explanation: A Security Baseline provides a set of minimum security standards and requirements that systems and applications must meet. It helps ensure that all components of an IT infrastructure are configured and maintained to a consistent security standard.

Answers

404. Answer: C

Explanation: In the Shared Responsibility Model, the cloud provider is responsible for securing the underlying cloud infrastructure, while the customer is responsible for securing their own data, applications, and access controls within the cloud environment.

405. Answer: B

Explanation: Intrusion Prevention Systems (IPS) are designed to detect and block malicious traffic in real-time based on predefined security policies. They provide an active defense mechanism to prevent attacks from reaching their target.

406. Answer: B

Explanation: SQL Injection attacks exploit vulnerabilities in web applications by injecting malicious SQL queries into input fields. This can allow attackers to access, modify, or delete data in a database.

407. Answer: C

Explanation: Role-Based Access Control (RBAC) assigns permissions to users based on their roles within an organization. This simplifies the management of user access by grouping permissions into roles rather than assigning them individually.

408. Answer: B

Explanation: Network segmentation involves dividing a network into separate segments to contain and limit the impact of a security breach. By isolating different segments, organizations can prevent attackers from moving laterally across the network and accessing critical systems.

409. Answer: B

Answers

Explanation: Time-based One-Time Passwords (TOTP) use a time-based algorithm to generate a unique password for each authentication attempt. This prevents replay attacks by ensuring that each password is valid only for a short period and cannot be reused.

410. **Answer: C**

Explanation: A Business Impact Analysis (BIA) is used to identify and prioritize the critical functions and resources necessary for an organization's continuity in the event of a disruption. It helps in understanding the potential impact of various types of disruptions and guides the development of effective recovery strategies.

411. **Answer: A**

Explanation: Transport Layer Security (TLS) is designed to secure communications over an unsecured network, such as the internet. It provides encryption, integrity, and mutual authentication between the client and server, ensuring secure data transmission.

412. **Answer: C**

Explanation: The Application Layer in a multi-tier architecture is responsible for implementing and enforcing user authentication and authorization mechanisms. It ensures that only authorized users can access specific application functionalities and data.

413. **Answer: A**

Explanation: Symmetric Key Encryption uses the same key for both encryption and decryption, making it efficient but requiring secure key distribution. Asymmetric Key Encryption uses a pair of keys (public and private) for encryption and decryption, enhancing security but generally being slower.

Answers

414. Answer: B

Explanation: Security Information and Event Management (SIEM) systems centralize the collection, monitoring, and analysis of security events and incidents from various sources. They enable organizations to detect, investigate, and respond to potential security threats in a coordinated manner.

415. Answer: A

Explanation: Defense in Depth involves using multiple layers of security controls and measures to protect against a wide range of threats. This strategy ensures that if one layer of defense is breached, other layers still provide protection, enhancing overall security.

416. Answer: B

Explanation: During the initial phase of an Incident Response Plan (IRP), the primary focus is on containing the incident to limit its impact. This involves isolating affected systems, stopping ongoing attacks, and preventing further damage before moving on to other response phases.

417. Answer: B

Explanation: The Principle of Least Privilege ensures that users are given the minimum level of access necessary to perform their job functions. This reduces the risk of accidental or malicious misuse of permissions and helps protect sensitive data.

418. Answer: C

Explanation: The Health Insurance Portability and Accountability Act (HIPAA) sets standards for the security and privacy of healthcare

Answers

information in the United States. It mandates specific measures for safeguarding patient data and ensuring its confidentiality and integrity.

About Our Products

About Our Products

Other products from VERSAtile Reads are:

 Elevate Your Leadership: The 10 Must-Have Skills

 Elevate Your Leadership: 8 Effective Communication Skills

 Elevate Your Leadership: 10 Leadership Styles for Every Situation

 300+ PMP Practice Questions Aligned with PMBOK 7, Agile Methods, and Key Process Groups – 2024

 Exam-Cram Essentials Last-Minute Guide to Ace the PMP Exam - Your Express Guide featuring PMBOK® Guide

 Career Mastery Blueprint - Strategies for Success in Work and Business

 Memory Magic: Unraveling the Secret of Mind Mastery

 CCNA Exam Cram: Essential Exam Success

 CISSP Fast Track Master: CISSP Essentials for Exam Success

 CISA Fast Track Master: CISA Essentials for Exam Success

About Our Products

 CISM Fast Track Master: CISM Essentials for Exam Success

 CCSP Fast Track Master: CCSP Essentials for Exam Success

 CLF-C02: AWS Certified Cloud Practitioner: Fast Track to Exam Success

 ITIL 4 Foundation Essentials: Fast Track to Exam Success

 CCNP Security Essentials: Fast Track to Exam Success

 Certified SCRUM Master Exam Cram Essentials

 Six Sigma Green Belt Exam Cram: Essentials for Exam Success

 Microsoft 365 Fundamentals: Fast Track to Exam Success

 CKA Essentials: Fast Track to Exam Success

 CompTIA ITF+ Exam Cram: Essential Exam Success

 TCA Exam Cram: Essential Exam Success

www.ingramcontent.com/pod-product-compliance
Lightning Source LLC
Chambersburg PA
CBHW062105220526
45471CB00010B/3600